# Railroad Equipment

HE
2236
S86

# Financing

By DONALD MACQUEEN STREET

Columbia University Press  New York  1959

*Library of Congress Catalog Card Number: 59-10085*

*Published 1959, Columbia University Press, New York*

*Published in Great Britain, Canada, India, and Pakistan
by the Oxford University Press
London, Toronto, Bombay, and Karachi*

*Manufactured in the United States of America*

*RAILROAD EQUIPMENT FINANCING*

*TO RUTH, in appreciation of the cheerful patience and unfailing encouragement without which this work never could have been completed*

# Acknowledgments

THE subject of this study was proposed to me by Professor James C. Bonbright, to whom thanks are due for the suggestion, for his sponsorship, and for most helpful advice and encouragement in connection with its preparation, revision, and presentation. Thanks are likewise due, and gratefully extended, to his associates, Professors B. H. Beckhart and Ernest W. Williams, Jr., for similar advice, encouragement, and suggestions, and to the staff of the library of Columbia University, particularly Mrs. Charlotte H. Sherr in the Law Library, for material provided and guidance given with unfailing cheerfulness and patience.

Outside the University, I have first to thank friends and former associates at the Guaranty Trust Company of New York, too numerous to mention individually, for material and research facilities provided, questions answered, and suggestions. Then I wish to thank Mr. Thomas O'Gorman FitzGibbon, of the firm of Davis Polk Wardwell Sunderland & Kiendl, for advice, guidance, and material in connection with legal phases of the study, and Mr. John Stevenson and his associates at Salomon Bros. & Hutzler for advice and material which were of immeasurable help in expediting the work. Thanks are due also to friends in other investment banking firms for their cheerful and generous cooperation, and to Mr. James T. Harrigan and his associates at The Hanover Bank, together with Mr. Frank H. Heiss of Kelley, Drye, Newhall and Maginness, counsel for that bank, for information and advice in connection with the New York, Ontario and Western litigation reviewed in Chapter IV. Further thanks are due to Mr. Hunter Holding, Second Vice President of The Equitable Life Assurance Society, for advice and information in connection with that company's leasing plan.

I also wish to thank Appleton-Century-Crofts for permission to quote copyrighted matter from Kenneth Duncan's *Equipment Obligations* and The Ronald Press Company for similar permission to quote from Arthur Stone Dewing's *A Study of Corporation Securities.*

I am indebted to my daughter, Mary S. Thorne, for the initial typing of my manuscript, mostly under circumstances where it would have been impossible to secure professional assistance.

Finally, I wish to express my gratitude to Salomon Bros. & Hutzler for financial aid which has helped to make the publication of this study possible.

DONALD MACQUEEN STREET

# Contents

| | | |
|---|---|---|
| I. | INTRODUCTION | 1 |
| II. | WHY DISTINCTIVE EQUIPMENT FINANCING? | 15 |
| III. | HISTORY OF EQUIPMENT FINANCING | 21 |
| IV. | LEGAL STATUS OF EQUIPMENT OBLIGATIONS | 44 |
| V. | EXPERIENCE IN RECEIVERSHIP AND REORGANIZATION | 69 |
| VI. | EQUIPMENT TRUST AGREEMENTS | 83 |
| VII. | CONDITIONAL SALE CONTRACTS | 104 |
| VIII. | LEASE ARRANGEMENTS | 124 |
| IX. | MARKETING EQUIPMENT OBLIGATIONS | 135 |
| X. | CONCLUSION | 150 |

*Appendix*

| | | |
|---|---|---|
| A. | FORM OF TRUST CERTIFICATE | 157 |
| B. | FORM OF DIVIDEND WARRANT | 161 |
| C. | FORM OF GUARANTY | 162 |
| D. | FORM OF CIRCULAR ON EQUIPMENT TRUST | 163 |
| | INDEX | 167 |

# *Tables*

*1* GROSS CAPITAL EXPENDITURES FOR ADDITIONS AND BETTERMENTS, AND ISSUE OF EQUIPMENT OBLIGATIONS, BY YEARS  4

*2* COMPARISON OF GROSS CAPITAL EXPENDITURES WITH CHARGES TO EARNINGS FOR DEPRECIATION, RETIREMENTS, AND AMORTIZATION OF DEFENSE PROJECTS (EQUIPMENT ONLY, IN ALL FOUR CASES) AND WITH EQUIPMENT OBLIGATIONS ISSUED  6

*3* COMPARISON OF FUNDED DEBT AND EQUIPMENT OBLIGATIONS OUTSTANDING  10

*4* RATIO OF CERTIFICATES OUTSTANDING AT START OF EACH YEAR TO ORIGINAL COST OF EQUIPMENT, ON VARIOUS ASSUMPTIONS AS TO DOWN PAYMENT AND MATURITY SCHEDULE  98

*RAILROAD EQUIPMENT FINANCING*

*CHAPTER I*

# Introduction

THIS study concerns the distinctive means which American railroads have developed to finance the acquisition of equipment, in the sense of rolling stock—cars and locomotives.

The standard work in the field is Duncan's,[1] published more than thirty years ago. Since that time we have had the experience of the depression and of the Second World War, the replacement of steam locomotives by diesel, new federal legislation and regulation, the development of such previously unimportant vehicles of finance as nonnegotiable conditional sale contracts and lease arrangements, and new marketing techniques. Smith made an ambitious study [2] some years ago, but that was concerned primarily with the legal factors, has never been published, and is already out of date. There have been recent useful articles by Adkins and Billyou, and by Stevenson,[3] but the time seems ripe for a full-scale survey, especially in view of the emergence of equipment financing as the chief source

[1] Kenneth Duncan, *Equipment Obligations* (New York, Appleton, 1924).

[2] Paul Smith, Jr., The Development of the Legal Status of American Railroad Equipment Securities (unpublished J.S.D. dissertation submitted at New York University, School of Law, March, 1950).

[3] Leonard D. Adkins, and DeForest Billyou, "Current Developments in Railroad Equipment Financing," *The Business Lawyer*, XII (1957),

of new investment capital for the railroads.[4] I propose to show the nature and extent of equipment financing, its background (historic, legal, and business), the techniques which have been developed for the benefit of the railroad and the protection of the investor, and the procedures and problems of marketing the obligations created.

Table 1 shows year by year, from 1921 through 1955, capital expenditures on equipment, total capital expenditures, and equipment obligations issued during the year. Equipment obligations may be defined as obligations (in the broadest sense, including contract obligations in non-negotiable form) to pay the balance of the purchase price of specified railroad equipment, secured by reserving title until payment is completed. Leases of equipment, which have become increasingly popular in the last few years, are not reported to the Interstate Commerce Commission or included in its statistics.

The magnitude of equipment expenditures, both in absolute amount and in relation to the total, is evident from the table. Only in the eleven years from 1925 through 1935 were expenditures for equipment less than half the total, falling to 21 percent or less in 1931–33. They were around 60 percent prior to 1925, and were over 60 percent in each of the last nine years, occasionally approaching 75 percent. Thus more funds have had to be provided, in

---

207. A publication of the Section of Corporation, Banking and Business Law of the American Bar Association.

John Stevenson, "Railroad Equipment Financing," *The Analysts Journal,* IX (No. 5, November, 1953), 27. A publication of The New York Society of Security Analysts, Inc.

[4] Since the war there has been almost no stock financing, and little bond financing save for refunding purposes.

*Introduction* 3

recent years, for equipment than for all other improvements combined; in some years two or three times as much.

A large part of these funds has come from charges to operating expenses for depreciation, retirements, and amortization of defense projects. In general, depreciation represents the annual accrual of a reserve over the life of the property, which is expected to offset (by the time when the property is retired from service) the difference between cost and scrap value. Retirement represents the excess of the loss on property retired in a particular year over the depreciation accrued to that time on that property. Amortization of defense projects represents an "accelerated depreciation" or more rapid write-off permitted on property certified to be necessary to the national defense. In view of the possibility that this property might lose part or all of its value near the end of the national emergency, and of the obvious fact that ability to charge it off rapidly (thereby reducing taxable income and consequently taxes payable) in a period of high taxes would be an inducement to the companies to make the investment, Congress authorized such charges by amendment to the revenue act in 1941 (Section 124). All three accounts represent non-cash charges to operating expenses (as opposed to the current cash outlay represented by wage payments, and purchases of fuel and other supplies) and therefore make funds available for other purposes, such as the purchase of new equipment.

In the thirty-five years from 1921 through 1955 such charges were sufficient to cover more than two thirds of gross capital expenditures on equipment. The relation

TABLE 1. GROSS CAPITAL EXPENDITURES OF CLASS I RAILWAYS IN THE UNITED STATES FOR ADDITIONS AND BETTERMENTS, AND ISSUE OF EQUIPMENT OBLIGATIONS, BY YEARS

(In millions of dollars)

|  | CAPITAL EXPENDITURES [a] | | Equipment Obligations Issued |
|---|---|---|---|
|  | Equipment | Total |  |
| 1921 | 320 | 557 | 62 [b] |
| 1922 | 246 | 429 | 128 |
| 1923 | 682 | 1,059 | 293 |
| 1924 | 494 | 875 | 229 |
| 1925 | 338 | 748 | 142 |
| 1926 | 372 | 885 | 131 |
| 1927 | 289 | 772 | 78 |
| 1928 | 224 | 677 | 88 |
| 1929 | 321 | 854 | 128 |
| 1930 | 328 | 873 | 117 |
| 1931 | 73 | 362 | 26 |
| 1932 | 36 | 167 | 9 |
| 1933 | 15 | 104 | 5 |
| 1934 | 92 | 213 | 78 |
| 1935 | 79 | 188 | 50 |
| 1936 | 159 | 299 | 77 |
| 1937 | 323 | 510 | 171 |
| 1938 | 115 | 227 | 27 |
| 1939 | 133 | 262 | 63 |
| 1940 | 272 | 429 | 131 |
| 1941 | 368 | 543 | 210 |
| 1942 | 349 | 535 | 93 [c] |
| 1943 | 256 | 454 | 89 |
| 1944 | 328 | 560 | 130 |
| 1945 | 315 | 563 | 121 |
| 1946 | 319 | 562 | 221 |
| 1947 | 566 | 865 | 415 |
| 1948 | 917 | 1,273 | 551 |
| 1949 | 981 | 1,312 | 507 |
| 1950 | 779 | 1,066 | 424 |
| 1951 | 1,051 | 1,414 | 704 [d] |
| 1952 | 935 | 1,341 | 606 |
| 1953 | 858 | 1,260 | 410 |
| 1954 | 499 | 820 | 274 |
| 1955 | 568 | 908 | 275 |

*Introduction* 5

varied widely from one period to another, however. Grouping the figures into five-year periods, as in Table 2, we see that depreciation and related charges were several times capital expenditures in 1931–35 (at about the depth of the depression), almost equalled expenditures from 1936 through 1940, and again exceeded them in 1941–45 (thanks to the accelerated amortization of the war period), but were well below expenditures in 1926–30 and were less than half of expenditures in the periods of heavy equipment purchases—1921–25 and 1946–55.

Even when depreciation charges greatly exceed the year's equipment purchases, much of the purchasing may be financed by other means. One reason is that the companies making the purchases may not be the ones which have depreciation funds available. The figures shown are the aggregates for all roads, so that an individual road

---

Sources: Figures for capital expenditures are taken from *Railroad Transportation: A Statistical Record, 1921–1955* (Washington, D.C., Bureau of Railway Economics, Association of American Railroads, 1956). Figures for equipment obligations issued are taken from *Statistics of Railways in the United States* [Statement 19A through 1937, Table 148 in subsequent years] (Washington, D.C., Interstate Commerce Commission).

[a] Represents total money outlay, without deductions for property retired.

[b] Perhaps incomplete; Statement 19A in different form from subsequent years.

[c] In this and subsequent years includes conditional sale contracts as listed in *Statistics of Railways,* Table 146-A.

[d] In this and subsequent years includes (from footnote to Table 148) those issued by receivers and bankruptcy trustees, and excludes down payment on conditional sale contracts; in previous years figure reported on such contracts represents entire purchase price, rather than deferred payments.

may find its own depreciation accruals short of proposed purchases in spite of a great excess in the aggregate figures. The more important reason, however, is that the depreciation charge does not set up a specific fund, earmarked for replacement and available for nothing else.

TABLE 2. COMPARISON OF GROSS CAPITAL EXPENDITURES OF CLASS I RAILWAYS IN THE UNITED STATES WITH CHARGES TO EARNINGS FOR DEPRECIATION, RETIREMENTS, AND AMORTIZATION OF DEFENSE PROJECTS (EQUIPMENT ONLY, IN ALL FOUR CASES) AND WITH EQUIPMENT OBLIGATIONS ISSUED

|  | Gross Capital Expenditures on Equipment | Depreciation, Retirements, Amortization of Defense Projects | Equipment Obligations Issued | Ratio of Obligations Issued to Capital Expenditures |
|---|---|---|---|---|
|  | (In millions of dollars) |  |  | (In percent) |
| 1921–25 | 2,068 | 918 | 852 | 41.2 |
| 1926–30 | 1,524 | 1,160 | 542 | 35.5 |
| 1931–35 | 295 | 989 | 168 | 57.0 |
| 1936–40 | 1,002 | 980 | 469 | 46.9 |
| 1941–45 | 1,616 | 2,170 | 642 | 39.7 |
| 1946–50 | 3,562 | 1,347 | 2,116 | 63.0 |
| 1951–55 | 3,911 | 1,796 | 2,269 | 58.0 |

Sources: Capital expenditures and equipment obligations issued compiled from Table 1. Depreciation, retirements, and amortization compiled from *Statistics of Railways* (Statement 37 through 1937, Table 95 in subsequent years).

It becomes part of the general funds of the company, available for any legitimate corporate purpose, and other purposes may be more pressing than the purchase of new equipment. In the depression, for instance, there was a general surplus of rolling stock, and a pressing need of funds for other purposes. Paying maturing obligations,

# Introduction

or even meeting operating deficits, might be more important than buying more cars and locomotives, or the funds might be needed to pay for improvements to which the road was committed and for which it could not raise money, under conditions then existing, by selling securities. Perhaps the funds could best be used for meeting maturing obligations, for retiring securities or acquiring property at bargain prices, or for building up working capital in preparation for future emergencies. Thus it may be good business for a road to finance its equipment purchases by the sale of equipment obligations, or even to lease equipment on favorable terms, and use the funds made available through depreciation charges to meet other needs for which financing would otherwise be difficult or impossible.

The last column of Table 1 shows the equipment obligations sold each year; the size and growth of the sales are evident in Table 1, and are still more striking in Table 2, where the figures are grouped into seven five-year periods. It is interesting to note that the ratio between equipment obligations sold and capital expenditures on equipment was almost as great in the depression years 1931–35, when capital expenditures were but a fraction of depreciation accruals, as in the decade of heavy expenditures since the war; in other words, equipment financing was the readiest means of raising capital whenever the railroads were pinched for cash, whether from reduced earnings during the depression or from increased capital requirements in the postwar period.

Figures on annual equipment financing are not available prior to 1920, when Section 20(a) of the Interstate

Commerce Act gave the Interstate Commerce Commission jurisdiction over the issue of carrier securities, but figures on the amount of equipment obligations outstanding are available for earlier years. When Rawle wrote the first authoritative treatise [5] on the subject in 1885, he estimated the outstanding amount at $40 million; when Duncan published his study in 1924 he estimated the outstanding amount at $800 million; when Smith prepared his admirable dissertation in 1950, he estimated the figure at $1,600 million; the 1955 total exceeded $2,500 million. (See Table 3.) Adding issues subsequent to 1955 (see the last sentence of the next paragraph) and issues of private car lines and Canadian railroads (see the last two paragraphs of this chapter), we find a grand total in excess of $3,000 million.

Nor is this simply an example of the inflation so general in economic statistics, particularly monetary statistics. Table 3 compares the outstanding equipment obligations with total railroad debt, at five-year intervals from 1890 to 1920, and annually thereafter. It will be seen that from approximately 1 percent of the total in 1890, equipment obligations increased to over 3 percent just before the First World War, to nearly 9 percent in the mid-twenties and (after a decline to less than 4 percent in consequence of limited equipment purchases in the thirties) to 8 percent around the end of the Second World War and to 25 percent in the last few years. Recent developments [6] have

[5] Francis Rawle, "Car Trust Securities," *American Bar Association Reports,* VIII (1885), 277–322.
[6] See below, Chapter IV.

*Introduction* 9

strengthened the legal status of such issues and investor confidence in them, and they seem destined to play a major role in railroad financing whenever equipment purchases are heavy. Since each issue matures serially over a period of not more than fifteen years, the average life of the obligations outstanding at any one time is less than fifteen years, and the total can be expected to run off rapidly with any cessation of equipment purchases. With substitution of diesel-electric power for steam approaching completion (in 1955 approximately 85 percent of freight service, 89 percent of passenger service, and 91 percent of switching service was performed by diesel-electric locomotives),[7] expenditures on motive power may decline, but General Motors is now urging the economies of replacing rather than overhauling the older units.[8] On freight cars expenditures seem likely to continue heavy; at the end of 1955 23 percent of all freight cars were more than thirty years old, and 38½ percent were more than twenty-five years old.[9] Equipment trust financing (not including conditional sale contracts) approximated $334,308,000 in 1956, $347,183,000 in 1957, and $158,950,000 in 1958.[10]

An important form of financing not covered in these figures is the leasing plan worked out in 1949 by The

[7] *Railroad Transportation: A Statistical Record, 1921–1955* (Washington, D.C., Bureau of Railway Economics, Association of American Railroads, 1956), p. 26.

[8] See below, Chapter VI.

[9] *Railroad Car Facts, 1955* (New York, American Railway Car Institute, 1956), p. 2.

[10] Figures supplied by John Stevenson, a partner of Salomon Bros. & Hutzler.

TABLE 3. COMPARISON OF FUNDED DEBT AND EQUIPMENT OBLIGATIONS OUTSTANDING OF ALL STEAM RAILWAYS IN THE UNITED STATES [a]

| End of Year [b] | Total Funded Debt | Equipment Obligations | Ratio of Equipment Obligations to Total Debt |
|---|---|---|---|
| | (In millions of dollars) | | (In percent) |
| 1890 | 4,575 | 49 | 1.11 |
| 1895 | 5,385 | 56 | 1.04 |
| 1900 | 5,645 | 60 | 1.07 |
| 1905 | 7,250 | 186 | 2.57 |
| 1910 | 10,303 | 353 | 3.42 |
| 1915 | 11,085 | 371 | 3.35 |
| 1920 | 11,255 | 653 | 5.80 |
| 1921 | 11,358 | 671 | 5.90 |
| 1922 | 11,502 | 720 | 6.26 |
| 1923 | 11,965 | 925 | 7.73 |
| 1924 | 12,381 | 1,057 | 8.55 |
| 1925 | 12,321 | 1,079 | 8.76 |
| 1926 | 12,384 | 1,097 | 8.88 |
| 1927 | 12,309 | 1,064 | 8.64 |
| 1928 | 12,303 | 980 | 7.98 |
| 1929 | 12,459 | 995 | 8.00 |
| 1930 | 12,771 | 984 | 7.72 |
| 1931 | 12,739 | 881 | 6.91 |
| 1932 | 12,789 | 763 | 5.96 |
| 1933 | 12,630 | 652 | 5.16 |
| 1934 | 12,454 | 621 | 4.99 |
| 1935 | 12,154 | 539 | 4.43 |
| 1936 | 12,031 | 502 | 4.16 |
| 1937 | 11,882 [c] | 555 | 4.68 |
| 1938 | 11,640 | 441 | 3.79 |
| 1939 | 11,420 | 426 | 3.73 |
| 1940 | 11,277 | 481 | 4.26 |
| 1941 | 11,209 | 625 | 5.57 |
| 1942 | 11,072 [d] | 711 [d] | 6.44 |
| 1943 | 10,650 [e] | 774 [e] | 7.26 |
| 1944 | 10,135 | 781 | 7.70 |
| 1945 | 9,437 | 773 | 8.19 |
| 1946 | 9,259 | 845 | 9.13 |
| 1947 | 9,132 | 1,087 | 11.90 |

Introduction

TABLE 3. (Continued)

| End of Year [b] | Total Funded Debt | Equipment Obligations | Ratio of Equipment Obligations to Total Debt |
|---|---|---|---|
| | (In millions of dollars) | | (In percent) |
| 1948 | 9,398 | 1,438 | 15.27 |
| 1949 | 9,495 | 1,711 | 18.07 |
| 1950 | 9,533 | 1,866 | 19.63 |
| 1951 | 9,791 | 2,301 | 23.50 |
| 1952 | 9,891 | 2,595 | 26.30 |
| 1953 | 9,841 | 2,695 | 27.32 |
| 1954 | 9,756 | 2,611 | 26.78 |
| 1955 | 9,764 | 2,539 | 26.01 |

Sources: Figures for funded debt and equipment obligations from *Statistics of Railways* (Table 141 in 1938 and subsequent years, with adjustments as indicated in footnotes; Statement 17 from 1922 through 1937; Statement 18 in 1920 and 1921; various statements in preceding years summarized in Duncan, *Equipment Obligations*, p. 23).

[a] Excluding switching and terminal companies.
[b] June 30 through 1915; December 31 thereafter.
[c] In this and subsequent years excludes funded debt matured unpaid.
[d] In this and subsequent years includes conditional sale contracts separately reported.
[e] In this and subsequent years includes equipment obligations separately reported (including conditional sale contracts and those issued by receivers or bankruptcy trustees: Tables 141A and 158).

Equitable Life Assurance Society. Under this plan, described in more detail in Chapter VIII, the Equitable purchases from the manufacturer freight cars or diesel-electric locomotives which the railroad wishes to acquire but does not think it advisable to finance on the usual terms, and simultaneously leases the equipment to the railroad at fixed rentals calculated to repay the investment, plus a reasonable interest return, over a fifteen-year period. The railroad undertakes to maintain, repair, and (when necessary) insure the equipment, and to settle under an agreed formula for any units lost or destroyed; it has the option of extending the lease, at a greatly reduced rental, at the end of the initial term, but at no time does it get title to the equipment. Provision is made for return of the property to Equitable, or upon its order, at the termination of the lease or of any extension, or, of course, in the event of default. To September 30, 1957, the Equitable had financed under this plan 22,192 freight cars, costing $129,938,000, and 507 diesel-electric locomotive units, costing $79,886,000, a total of $209,824,000.[11]

There is a large amount of rolling stock, particularly refrigerator cars and tank cars, owned not by the railroad corporation but by subsidiary corporations or others, collectively known as private car lines. In the case of refrigerator cars, the roads have been making increasing use of such private lines. At the end of 1922 the number of refrigerator cars owned by the Class I carriers approached that owned by the private car lines (63,454 vs. 67,694),[12] while at the end of 1955 the roads owned only 19,147 and the private car lines 104,568.[13] In the case of tank cars the decline in railroad ownership over the same period has been less spectacular, from 9,952 to 6,731, but at both dates private car lines were the chief owners, having 124,632 in 1922 and 150,536 in 1955.

[11] Letter to the writer (December 10, 1957) from Hunter Holding, Second Vice-President of the Equitable Life Assurance Society of the United States.
[12] *Statistics of Railways,* 1922, pp. xvi, viii; other 1922 figures from same source.
[13] *Ibid.,* 1955, tables 22A, 181; other 1955 figures from same source, except as otherwise indicated.

*Introduction* 13

Of the "private" refrigerator cars, about 75 percent [14] belong to companies which are controlled through stock ownership by one or more railroads. It is interesting to note the transfer of more than 22,000 cars to such companies in 1922 [15] and 1923,[16] perhaps in part to avoid Interstate Commerce Commission jurisdiction over railroad security issues under Section 20(a), which was added to the Interstate Commerce Act in 1920.[17] Railroad ownership appears to be far less extensive, perhaps negligible, in tank car lines and in other private car operations.

The aggregate of such private car ownership, including the refrigerator and tank cars previously discussed, has increased from 226,604 at the end of 1922 to 291,995 at the end of 1955, during a period when the number of cars owned by the railroads themselves was declining from 2,293,389 to 1,698,801. Thus private cars amounted to 15 percent of the total (railroad and private) at the end of 1955, against 9 percent at the end of 1922. This results from the relative increase in special equipment (refrigerator cars, railroad and private, represented 6.2 percent of all freight carrying cars in 1955 against 5.2 percent in 1922, and tank cars 7.9 percent against 5.3 percent) plus the railroad policy of leaving the supply of such cars largely to private owners (including railroad subsidiaries in the case of refrigerator cars).[18]

[14] 80,517 at end of 1955: *Railroad Transportation*, p. 2.
[15] *Statistics of Railways*, 1922, p. xvi.
[16] *Ibid.*, 1923, p. xiv.
[17] See below, Chapter IV.
[18] Percentages calculated from figures quoted within the last three paragraphs.

Equipment obligations against such private cars are not included in Table 3. Interstate Commerce Commission jurisdiction over such companies is very limited, and the financial data are quite unsatisfactory. However, figures compiled by one of the leading underwriters give a total of more than $200 million equipment obligations outstanding at the end of 1954 for five of the largest private car lines.[19]

Equipment obligations have likewise been extensively used in Canada. At the end of 1955 the two principal Canadian systems (the government-owned Canadian National and the privately owned Canadian Pacific had outstanding $39,395,000 and $61,379,000 respectively,[20] a total of more than $100 million.

[19] Pacific Fruit Express, Fruit Growers Express, Western Fruit Express, Merchants Despatch, and General American Transportation. (Letter to the writer [December 2, 1955] from John Stevenson.)

[20] *Moody's Manual of Investments: Transportation,* 1956 (New York, Moody's Investors Service), pp. 1018, 1045.

CHAPTER II

# Why Distinctive Equipment Financing?

THE inability of the typical railroad to give a first mortgage on its line as security for further borrowing is perhaps the first reason historically, and still one of the strongest practically, for financing based on the security of the equipment—i.e., the particular lot of rolling stock being purchased. Usually the railroad, through most of its history, has been covered by a closed first mortgage—i.e., one under which the authorized limit of bonds has already been issued. The New York Central main lines, for instance, are subject to first mortgages of $100 million east of Buffalo and $50 million west of that city, to second liens approximating $40 million, and a third lien of $69 million; any further mortgage borrowing must be junior to this mass of debt, almost none of which is subject to retirement for another forty years![1] The main lines of the Southern Railway, to cite another typical case, are covered by a $120 million mortgage under which no more bonds may be issued (with minor exceptions) and

[1] Calculations by the writer from data in *Moody's Manual of Investments: Transportation*, 1955 (New York, Moody's Investors Service), pp. 970–73.

the bonds now outstanding are not subject to retirement until 1994.[2] Small wonder then that borrowers have sought and lenders have insisted on getting, when possible, some form of security better than a mortgage which would necessarily be subject to such enormous prior claims. Even if a company is in a position to issue additional first mortgage bonds, the value of those bonds is necessarily tied up with the general credit of the company. The value of a railroad, and therefore of the bonds secured by mortgage on it, is dependent on its earning power. Capital invested in roadway and structures is irretrievably sunk in the enterprise; its value can be realized only by making the railroad pay. The scrap value of rails and wire, switches and tracks and signals, is comparatively low and realizable only at considerable labor cost; ties and ballast and telegraph poles have no scrap value worth mentioning; a right of way—unless one should strike oil!—is useful only for another railroad, a highway, or a pipe line. Even these values would be realizable only on the assumption that the company, or the bondholders after foreclosure, are permitted to scrap the property, which is rarely the case. Authority to discontinue operation of an unprofitable line is difficult to obtain, in the face of the vigorous opposition invariably offered by the very community which has been unwilling to use the road enough to make its operation profitable! Even sale of the property, or segments of it, to another road for continued operation requires official sanction that may be impossible to secure, or at best long delayed.

[2] *Ibid.*, p. 682.

## Distinctive Equipment Financing

A first lien on standard rolling stock avoids these difficulties. If it is indeed the first claim on a particular lot of equipment, which is simply a matter of setting up the financing along the right lines, under well-established statutes and precedents,[3] existing bondholders have no claim —or at most a junior claim, which cannot jeopardize the interests of those who supply the present funds. As the equipment is standard,[4] it can be used by almost any railroad; its value does not depend on the earning power of the present borrower. It can be delivered to any purchaser with a minimum of expense, under its own power in the case of locomotives (other than electric locomotives) or by incorporation in a train in the case of cars.[5]

Moreover, the right to enforce this lien on equipment with a minimum of delay, and with reasonable compensa-

---
[3] See Chapter IV, below.

[4] Standard as here used implies standard gauge—i.e. adapted to operation on the 56½ inch distance between rails to which American railroads (with minor exceptions of decreasing importance) have been built or adapted for many years; standard in fitting and equipment, so that they can be coupled with other cars and operated under routine procedures; reasonably standard in size and character—i.e., if adapted for a particular service (e.g., refrigerator cars), it must be one of which there are various users.

[5] One of the classic cases of default on equipment obligations, the Denver and Rio Grande in 1885 (see Chapter V, below) involved narrow gauge equipment, which presented both the problem of where to find a buyer at a time when roads were rapidly being converted to standard gauge, and the further problem of how to make delivery to any buyer whose narrow gauge lines did not connect with those of the Denver; the equipment would have to be shipped, rather than steamed or towed, over the standard gauge mileage between. A similar problem of delivery arises in the case of trolley cars or rapid transit equipment; though standard in gauge, they are not adapted to incorporation into an ordinary train, and if sold in another community must be shipped rather than towed to the purchaser.

tion for any such delay, is established by statutory enactment and a long line of judicial decisions.[6] In the case of equipment obligations perhaps more than in that of any other corporate security, the formidable language of the document means what it says, and sets forth rights which are actually enforceable just about as stated.[7]

The holder is further protected by the practice of setting up the obligation in serial form, payable over a period of years well within the equipment's anticipated life span. Thus equipment obligations offer a unique opportunity of borrowing on the best security, the value of which is not tied to the fortune of the particular borrower, in a range of maturities (ordinarily from one to fifteen years) appealing to various types of investors. Small wonder that these obligations are marketable in immense quantity, and provide the cheapest means of financing for any railroad which has not a literal surfeit of cash.[8]

From a technical standpoint, perhaps the most distinctive feature of equipment financing is the means taken to assure that it is indeed the first claim on a particular

[6] See below, Chapter IV.

[7] Procedural problems presented by state statutes governing the sale of property repossessed under conditional sale contracts are not comparable with the obstacles which the Bankruptcy Act presents to the enforcement of mortgage liens, and did not prevent the sale of Florida East Coast and New York, Ontario and Western equipment. (See below, Chapter V.)

[8] In every year since 1933 the average rate on equipment financing has been less (frequently one quarter to one half less) than on other debt financing (U.S. Interstate Commerce Commission, *Statistics of Railways,* Table 148). For a more extended discussion of the investment status of equipment obligations and the markets for them, see Chapter IX, below.

## Distinctive Equipment Financing

lot of equipment, as stated above. Railroad mortgages ordinarily contain an "after acquired property" clause, conveying to the mortgage trustee, for the benefit of the mortgage bondholders, not only title to the property which the road has at the time, but "the estate, right, title and interest which the Company may hereafter acquire in or to any other property." [9] The existence of mortgages carrying such clauses means that the railroad itself cannot give the equipment trustee a satisfactory title to any rolling stock the railroad owns. As soon as the railroad company acquires ownership, even temporarily, the lien of the existing mortgages attaches to the property, and all the company can give to the equipment trustee is a junior lien, subject to the existing mortgages and ob- viously unsatisfactory to those who are financing the equipment. To avoid this, a way must be found to give the equipment trustee title before the railroad company acquires, in Dewing's picturesque phrase, "even a shadow of a title." [10] This is accomplished by reserving title to the equipment, through lease or conditional sale, until payment in full is completed. The railroad company acquires the right to use and operate the equipment, but the builder conveys title directly to the trustee or other representative of those doing the financing, or reserves it to himself if doing his own financing, and any ownership by the railroad begins only when all the conditional payments have been completed. Some of the financing, notably

[9] Illinois Central Railroad Company Consolidated Mortgage dated November 1, 1949.
[10] Arthur Stone Dewing, *A Study of Corporation Securities* (New York, The Ronald Press Company, 1934), p. 369.

the Equitable lease plan,[11] may be leases in fact as well as form, carrying no implication of eventual ownership by the railroad company; the important thing is that whether the form is frankly a conditional sale, a conditional sale disguised as a lease,[12] or a straight lease, the investor is protected by reservation of title for his benefit; not by conveyance of title from borrower (or lessee) to trustee, but by reservation of title before it ever reaches the borrower (or lessee).

[11] See p. 9, above, and Chapter VIII.

[12] The so-called Philadelphia Plan. (See Chapters III and VI, below.)

*CHAPTER III*

# History of Equipment Financing

ACCORDING to Smith,[1] the first distinctive equipment financing was undertaken in 1839, when "The Proprietors of the Locks and Canals Company" at Lowell, Massachusetts, built several locomotives for the Baltimore and Susquehanna Rail Road Company, delivering them to the president of the road, who acted as agent for the seller, under an agreement by which title was to remain in the seller until the notes accepted in payment had been fully paid. This was within a decade of the historic day in December, 1830, when "The Best Friend of Charleston" became the first locomotive to haul a train along an American track.

In March, 1842, the same "Proprietors" entered into an agreement with the Philadelphia and Reading Railroad Company whereby the title to six hundred coal car assemblies was assigned to two individual trustees for the benefit of the builder. The trustees were to repossess and sell the equipment should the railroad fail to meet its obligation.[2] The purchase price was payable by reserving twenty-two and a half cents from the freight of every ton

[1] Paul Smith, Jr., The Development of the Legal Status of American Railroad Equipment Securities (unpublished J.S.D. dissertation, School of Law, New York University, 1950), p. 14.
[2] *Ibid.*, p. 15.

transported in the cars, to be applied to the purchase price until the latter was paid in full.[3]

In 1845 the Schuylkill Navigation Company adopted a plan for the acquisition of barges, and subsequently of cars, which Rawle mentions as "the germ of the modern idea of a car trust." He may have described it thus because he was not familiar with the cases just mentioned, or because it brought in specifically the idea of lease, the earlier ones being undisguised conditional sales.

The Board of Managers of the Schylkill Navigation Company negotiated a loan for the purpose of "constructing or purchasing barges, the construction and use of the barges to be controlled by the board," but "the ownership to be vested in three trustees, to be held as security for the payment of the loan." Afterwards the purchase of cars was included in the scheme. The bonds issued for the loan bore interest, and the principal was payable in ten annual installments. Under the arrangement made the trustees were to transfer the barges and cars to the company when the loan was fully repaid. . . . The trustees executed a deed of trust upon these terms, and "leased" the barges to the company "for a rent depending on the clear profit that might be derived from their use on the canal" and "leased" the cars to the company for a nominal consideration.

In 1848 a new arrangement was made by which the trustees were authorized to sell the barges from time to time for the benefit of the trust, and to "grant the use" of the cars to the Navigation Company on condition that it would pay the trustees all their expenses for repairing, etc., and would put them

[3] George S. Gibb, "Three Early Railroad Equipment Contracts," *Bulletin of the Business Historical Society,* XXI (February, 1947), 15.

## History of Equipment Financing

in funds to pay the principal and interest of outstanding bonds.[4]

Rawle[5] cites the "Railroad Car Trust of Philadelphia" as "the earliest . . . car trust of the kind now commonly found." He credits the idea to Edward W. Clark, president of the Lehigh Coal and Navigation Company, and the working of the legal details to Charles Gibbons, of the Philadelphia bar, explaining the necessity of the device in these terms:

Under the decisions in Pennsylvania, which held the retention of title in the vendor under a conditional sale of a chattel to be invalid as against third parties, the contract could not safely be drawn in the form of a conditional sale, and the draftsman was therefore obliged to base the contract upon the idea of a bailment [6] with an option in the vendee to purchase the cars at the termination of the contract, following, to a certain extent, the case of Lehigh Coal and Navigation Company vs. Field, 8 Watts & Sargeant, 232. In that case, a boatman in the employ of the Navigation Company agreed to purchase a canal boat, and to pay for it in installments, but the boat was to remain the property of the company until paid for; the boatman continued to act as the servant of the company, though in possession of the boat, which he operated on the line of the company's canal. It was held that

[4] Francis Rawle, "Car Trust Securities," *American Bar Association Reports*, VIII (1885), 277–322. See footnotes on p. 322.

[5] *Ibid.*, p. 277.

[6] "A delivery of goods or money by one person to another in trust, for some special purpose, upon a contract, expressed or implied, that the trust shall be faithfully executed." Blackstone, as quoted in *Webster's New International Dictionary*, Second Edition Unabridged (Springfield, Mass., A. and C. Merriam Co., 1954).

the title to the boat was both ostensibly and really in the hands of the company, and that it was not subject to levy by the execution creditors of the vendee. It may be added, that while retention of title in the vendor under a conditional sale has always been held invalid as to third parties in Pennsylvania, yet contracts in the nature of a bailment, with an option in the bailee to purchase at the termination of the contract, have always been upheld, even though the so-called hire was in reality the payment of the purchase-money by installments.

From this has developed directly the Philadelphia Plan, under which practically all equipment trust certificates are now issued. The railroad contracts with the manufacturer for the purchase of equipment, but takes care not to acquire it (or make payment for it) directly. Instead, the manufacturer delivers the bill of sale to the trustee, receiving payment from the latter upon delivery of the bill and accompanying documents, particularly the railroad's acceptance of the equipment. Funds with which to make payment have come to the trustee from the railroad (in the form of an "advance rental," ordinarily around 20 percent, representing its down payment on the purchase) and from the underwriters (representing the principal amount of the certificates, which they have undertaken to sell, for the balance of the purchase price, ordinarily 80 percent). The certificates, issued by the trustee in $1,000 denomination, represent undivided interests in the trust, mature serially (ordinarily in from one to fifteen years), carry "dividends" at a rate stipulated in the trust agreement, and are guaranteed as to principal and dividends by the railroad company. The rail-

## History of Equipment Financing

road undertakes to pay as rental sums sufficient to cover principal and dividends on the certificates; to maintain, operate, repair, and (when necessary) insure the equipment; to pay all taxes; and to do everything necessary to protect the trustee's title. Although the certificates are issued by the trustee, it is stipulated that principal and dividends are payable only from the rentals, and the certificates are recognized, in law and practice, as the obligations of the railroad company. The railroad is stated to hold the equipment only as lessee, and in the event of default in the rental, the trustee has the right to demand return of the equipment, which will presumably be worth substantially more than the balance of certificates outstanding, in view of the original down payment and subsequent maturities, which are scheduled at a rate exceeding the anticipated depreciation of the equipment. Only on completion of the rental payments is the trustee to give the railroad title to the equipment.

Rawle remarks that this plan was adopted not only by other railroad companies in Pennsylvania, but by many in other states, even ". . . in jurisdictions where conditional sales were valid and the more appropriate medium of a conditional sale might have been employed with entire safety and greater propriety." [7]

The obvious alternative of financing by notes based on a conditional sale, sometimes called "The New York Plan," appears to have been most popular in the first quarter of the present century.[8] Of the Equipment Trusts of

[7] Rawle, "Car Trust Securities," p. 278.
[8] Smith, Development of Legal Status, p. 22.

January 15, 1920,[9] which were created to secure nearly $350 million notes and certificates delivered by the railroads to the United States Railroad Administration in payment for equipment purchased during the period of government control and operation incident to the First World War, only the Pennsylvania Railroad agreement was under the Philadelphia Plan. All of the others, representing about eighty-five percent of the dollar total, were conditional sale agreements.

Under the conditional sale plan, the trustee made payment to the manufacturer with funds supplied by the railroad (the down payment) and by the underwriters. The securities which the underwriters sold to raise these funds were not trust certificates, as in the Philadelphia Plan, but notes of the railroad secured by reservation of title in the trustee for the benefit of the noteholders until the notes should be paid in full. The covenants of the railroad company, and the rights and remedies of trustee and noteholder in the event of default, were similar to those under the Philadelphia Plan. The agreements frequently characterized the installment payments as rental and the railroad's possession as a lessee's, but this appears to have been mere window dressing, presumably to borrow some of the prestige of the Philadelphia Plan; the transaction was a conditional sale, practically undisguised.

It is not clear why this conditional sale plan should have faded out, after a quarter century in which the Philadelphia Plan ran a very poor second. Since the adoption by

[9] Kenneth Duncan, *Equipment Obligations* (New York, Appleton, 1924), pp. 68 ff.

## History of Equipment Financing

all states of legislation validating conditional sales,[10] only Dewing seems to think that the Philadelphia Plan continues to have substantial legal advantages. We have already quoted Rawle's view on the "entire safety and greater propriety" of the conditional sale form in jurisdictions where such sales are valid. Smith observes that it "is more realistic and certainly simpler";[11] Duncan indicates a distinct preference for it;[12] only Dewing argues that statutory enactment is not law, and not (until tested by litigation and judicial construction) a satisfactory substitute for the established judicial backing of the Philadelphia Plan—which, he argues, gives the railroad "not even a shadow of an equitable or legal title," as opposed to "at least a shadow of an equitable title" under conditional sale.[13] My own conclusion is entirely in agreement with Smith's [14] that the major objection to use of the conditional sale plan is the high esteem with which its alternative is regarded; apparently the Philadelphia Plan has just enough legerdemain to capture the imagination of the investor, who finds it easier to understand the idea that the railroad simply operates the equipment under lease while the trust certificates are outstanding than to grasp the subtleties of retaining title under conditional sale.

Equipment bonds, secured by mortgage on rolling stock,

[10] *Ibid.*, p. 155.
[11] Smith, Development of Legal Status, p. 23.
[12] Duncan, *Equipment Obligations,* p. 38.
[13] Arthur Stone Dewing, *A Study of Corporation Securities* (New York, The Ronald Press Company, 1934), p. 370.
[14] Smith, Development of Legal Status, p. 23.

are generally recognized as weaker than either equipment trust certificates or conditional sale notes.[15] Smith says "a chattel mortgage . . . is precisely what an investor in railroad equipment securities does not want," pointing out the hazard of finding such a lien impaired by the after-acquired-property clause of some other mortgage.[16] This could presumably be avoided by making the chattel mortgage a purchase money obligation—i.e., one coming into existence simultaneously with the railroad's acquisition of title, and thus before existing mortgages have a chance to attach—or by what Dewing mentions [17] as the Canadian device of having the manufacturer place a lien on the equipment before it is sold to the railroad company. Under present legislation, a sounder objection would seem to be that such obligations would not share the protection which Section 77 of the Bankruptcy Act gives to the title of any owner to "rolling stock equipment leased or conditionally sold to the debtor, and any right of such owner to take possession of such property in compliance with the provisions of any such lease or conditional sale contract." [18] An equipment bond resting on mortgage security would be one of the debtor's obligations subject to the general provisions of that act, including the power of the court to enjoin enforcement of the creditors' contractual rights,

---

[15] Dewing, *Corporation Securities,* p. 360; Duncan, *Equipment Obligations,* pp. 180 ff.; Smith, Development of Legal Status, pp. 9 ff.

[16] Smith, Development of Legal Status, p. 9.

[17] Dewing, *Corporation Securities,* p. 348, footnote.

[18] 49 *Stat.* 911 (1935); 11 U.S.C. 205 (1952)—last sentence of subsection (j).

## History of Equipment Financing

or to make bankruptcy trustee's certificates a prior lien on the mortgaged property.

Conditional sale contracts, under which the lender is protected by reservation of title as in the conditional sale plan described above, but in which the obligation is expressed in the contract itself without accompanying notes, have become increasingly important in recent years. The amount of such financing, first separately reported in 1942 at approximately $34 million, increased to approximately $413 million in 1951, and in both that year and 1952 substantially exceeded the issue of equipment trust certificates.[19] The reasons for this are twofold: convenience to the borrower, and availability of lenders able and willing to supply such funds without receiving a negotiable instrument.

Conveniences to the borrower are numerous. He does not have to obtain Interstate Commerce Commission approval.[20] He avoids the expense of having $1,000 certificates and accompanying coupons engraved, executed, and delivered. Underwriting expense is reduced or eliminated, since the contract is placed with one lender, or at most a few lenders, perhaps without any underwriter whatever; also reduced or eliminated are trustee's fees, and perhaps some of the legal expense. Sometimes a conditional sale contract contains provisions (e.g., for optional redemption, or for the loan to run only from the dates when the

[19] U.S. Interstate Commerce Commission, *Statistics of Railways*, Tables 148 and 146-A.

[20] See below, pp. 62–64.

various units of equipment are actually completed and delivered) which might be difficult to negotiate with an underwriter who is planning to beat the bushes for eventual purchasers, or which would be likely to discourage (if only because they represent a departure from standard practice) competitive bidders who do not expect to make at best more than a nominal profit on the deal.

Lenders able and willing to dispense with negotiability have appeared with the growth of institutional investors— e.g., life insurance companies and pension funds—of such a character that their investments are likely to be held to maturity, and with the accumulation of funds in great metropolitan banks which, in periods when the demand for money was slack and seemed likely to continue so, were actively looking for "term loans"—i.e., loans whose maturity extends beyond the period of months ordinarily associated with commercial bank credit, to installments over a period of several years. The fact that these contracts are not negotiable in form does not mean that the funds are irrevocably committed until the maturity date; they can, if necessary, be assigned and sold like other assets, although not designed for that purpose, as are bearer instruments which pass by delivery.

Fundamentally, the conditional sale contract is comparatively simple. The railroad, the lender, and the builder enter into three-cornered agreements under which, upon acceptance of the rolling stock by the railroad, the lender makes payment to the builder and receives title directly from him, to be held until the railroad has paid the deferred installments of the purchase price. Provisions

## History of Equipment Financing

for the protection of the loan are similar to those already discussed in connection with the Philadelphia Plan and the conditional sale plan, and I know of no one who disputes Stevenson's dictum that "conditional sale contracts occupy just as strong a position as Philadelphia Plan certificates." [21] A more extended discussion of such contracts, and the problems that may arise from having not one but several lenders, will be found in Chapter VII below.

In connection with the First World War, the federal government took over control and operation of the railroads of the United States from December 26, 1917, to March 1, 1920. During this period heavy purchase of equipment became necessary, the government advancing the necessary funds under Section 6 of the act approved March 21, 1918,[22] and accepting in payment equipment obligations under the Railroad Motive Power and Equipment Act of the following year.[23] Those obligations, under agreements dated January 15, 1920, with the Guaranty Trust Company of New York as trustee, were issued to a total approaching $350 million, by approximately eighty individual roads. There was no joint liability, each road paying for the equipment (or the pending orders) which it took over on termination of federal control. All matured serially over a fifteen year period, carried interest at 6 percent, were issued under the conditional sale plan except for the use of the Philadelphia Plan in the case of the

[21] John Stevenson, "Railroad Equipment Financing," *The Analysts Journal*, IX (No. 5, November, 1953), 29.
[22] 40 *Stat.* 455.  [23] 41 *Stat.* 359.

Pennsylvania Railroad, and were issued for approximately the full cost of the equipment.

The experience of the government with these obligations was better than might have been expected from the dubious credit of some of the borrowers, the absence of down payments, and the cost of equipment built during or immediately after the war.

During 1920 the market level of interest rates was such as to make 6 percent obligations quite unsalable; Atlantic Coast Line, Louisville and Nashville, New York Central, Norfolk and Western, Northern Pacific, and Pennsylvania all had to pay 7 percent on equipment obligations or other amply secured bonds sold in the spring of 1920.[24] During the following year, however, interest rates declined to such a point as to create a demand for the notes of some of the stronger roads, at the price of par for which the government held them, and on September 12, 1921, the government announced the sale of $7,500,000, maturing serially from 1928 through 1935, to Kuhn, Loeb and Company. These notes were stated to have been bought for investment and do not appear to have been reoffered, publicly at any rate, but within the next ten days further sales were announced, to syndicates of investment bankers (at least one of which resold promptly through public offering at prices to yield from 5.75 percent to 5.80 percent), to the Prudential Insurance Company (presumably for investment), and to others, to a total of

---

[24] *The Commercial and Financial Chronicle,* New York, CX, 2859 (April 10, 1920), pp. 1526–27; 2863 (May 8, 1920), pp. 1972–73; 2864 (May 15, 1920), pp. 2075–76.

## History of Equipment Financing

$63,482,600.[25] Further sales in subsequent months brought the total to $164,226,100, or about half the original issue (allowing for the reduction effected by the January 15, 1921, maturity).[26]

The agreements contained a provision [27] whereby later maturities could be subordinated in order to facilitate sale of the earlier, but this appears never to have been used. Instead, in 1922, when the War Finance Corporation, which had been negotiating the sales for the government, came to the conclusion that subordination of part would be necessary or desirable in order to facilitate further sales, supplemental agreements were executed subordinating such part of each maturity (actually one third) as the holder (i.e., the government) should request.[28] This so strengthened the position of the unsubordinated notes that in the fourth week of January, 1922, the government was able to announce sales exceeding $50,000,000.[29]

As the year proceeded, buyers were found not only for the unsubordinated notes, but for the better names among the subordinated.[30] The annual report of the Director General of Railroads summarizes transactions to the end of the year as follows:

[25] *Ibid.*, CXIII, 2935 (September 24, 1921), pp. 1324–25.

[26] *Ibid.*, CXIV, 2952 (January 21, 1922), p. 269.

[27] Article 13 of Pennsylvania agreement (Article 11 of other agreements) as quoted by Duncan, *Equipment Obligations,* pp. 73–75.

[28] *The Commercial and Financial Chronicle,* CXIV, 2953 (January 28, 1922), p. 374.

[29] *Ibid.*

[30] E.g., $3,283,800 Chesapeake and Ohio and $2,344,500 Chicago, Rock Island and Pacific. *The Commercial and Financial Chronicle,* CXIV, 2971 (June 3, 1922), p. 2431.

The total amount of these equipment trust notes taken by the director general was $346,556,750. Of this amount, $33,298,200 was collected on the maturity dates of January 15, 1921 ($23,103,650) and January 15, 1922 ($10,194,550) and in addition to these amounts of principal collected the Railroad Administration has sold, at the price of par and accrued interest to date of delivery $274,009,350 of these notes, $133,811,650 of this amount being sold during the calendar year 1922. . . . The Railroad Administration still holds . . . $39,249,200 of these notes.[31]

Exhibit 5 attached to the report (p. 21) shows that all of this balance on hand consisted of subordinated notes. The report for 1924 (p. 29) shows the balance on hand reduced to $5,919,500, and the report for 1932 summarizes the transactions in the following sentence: ". . . The total amount of such notes acquired was $346,556,750 of which $346,422,350 have been paid at maturity or sold to private investors, leaving a balance on hand January 1, 1932 of $134,400."[32] This balance, which was subordinated notes of Minneapolis and St. Louis Railroad Company, was paid as due, $33,600 each January 15, 1932 through 1935, thus getting the taxpayers out with 6 percent interest and no loss of principal.

The progressive decline in interest rates, which made the 6 percent coupon increasingly attractive, was one factor in creating a market for the notes. Reduction of the ratio of notes to cost of equipment, as earlier installments matured and were paid, was another. A most important factor was the improvement in railroad earnings

---

[31] 67th Congress, 4th session, House Document #546.
[32] 73d Congress, 1st session, House Document #40.

## History of Equipment Financing

and credit. Finally, there was a growing realization that the cost of new equipment was not going to be greatly reduced within the next few years [33] and that the revival of traffic, which was itself a major factor in restoring railroad earnings and credit, assured a good demand for the comparatively new equipment securing the notes.

So much for the experience of the government. How did the investors fare? The government's success in collecting its last holdings—the subordinated notes of Minneapolis and St. Louis, a road in receivership from 1923—suggests that the purchasers of the other obligations should have fared pretty well, and such was indeed the case. The records of Guaranty Trust Company of New York, trustee of all the issues, show that the great majority were paid when due, despite the financial difficulties of some of the borrowers. Twelve were called for retirement at 103 between 1923 and 1928. Six receivership or bankruptcy cases [34] involved defaults (generally only with the last few maturities, at the depth of the depression) which are reviewed in Chapter V; in none of these did the settlement involve substantial permanent loss.

In the past, special corporations have sometimes been formed to finance equipment purchases.[35] Some of these were in more or less permanent form, taking the buyer's

[33] Most of the notes had matured and been retired by the time the great depression of the 1930s brought a real reduction in the cost of capital goods.

[34] Atlanta, Birmingham and Atlantic; Rock Island; Norfolk Southern; Seaboard Air Line; St. Louis–San Francisco; Wabash.

[35] Duncan, *Equipment Obligations,* pp. 38–42; Smith, Development of Legal Status, pp. 7–8.

obligation for each lot of equipment and selling their own obligations to the public; others were set up to finance a particular deal, perhaps by selling preferred stock the dividend and sinking fund on which was assured by the railroad's "rental" payments for the equipment. They have chiefly an historical interest now, and Smith [36] points out quite rightly the legislative obstacles now existing: the railroad would need the consent of the Interstate Commerce Commission,[37] and if the securities were to be offered to the public they in turn would have to be registered with the Securities and Exchange Commission. These might not be insuperable obstacles if the equipment corporation would serve a useful purpose; revision of the statute might be difficult if not impossible, but experience both with conditional sale contracts and private car line equipment obligations has demonstrated a vast market for the private placement of well-secured issues.[38] Thus it may be interesting to review briefly the most ambitious of these projects, organized shortly after the First World War.

National Railway Service Corporation was the brain child of S. Davies Warfield, president of Seaboard Air Line Railway Company and of the National Association of Owners of Railroad Securities, who associated with himself as directors representatives of leading insurance

[36] Smith, *ibid.*

[37] Unless it neither issued nor directly guaranteed the securities; a mere contractual obligation might escape Commission jurisdiction as conditional sale contracts do now.

[38] See below, Chapter VIII (National Equipment Leasing, General Motors, and Alco Products), and IX.

## History of Equipment Financing

companies and other financial institutions. Incorporating in Maryland with nominal capital, they obtained recognition from the Interstate Commerce Commission as an agency to or through which loans could be made to carriers under the $300 millions revolving fund established by Section 210 of the Transportation Act of 1920 for the purpose of emergency aid to carriers, of which the Commission indicated that a large part could be used to aid in equipment purchases. The purpose was to facilitate the purchases by pooling the credit of the participating railroads, and to effect further economies through a unified control and pooling of the financing, inspecting, rebuilding, and repair of equipment and other joint facilities.

The Service Corporation established an Equipment Trust, Conditional Sale Basis, with Guaranty Trust Company of New York as trustee, and an Equipment Trust, Lease Basis, with Bankers Trust Company as trustee. Under each, Prior Lien Certificates at a 7 percent rate were to be issued to 60 percent of the cost of the equipment, and Deferred Lien Certificates at a 6 percent rate for the balance. The Prior Lien Certificates were to be sold to institutional investors and the Deferred Lien Certificates to the government against advances from the revolving fund; to give further protection to those advances the railroad delivered as additional collateral such further assets as it might have available and the government be willing to accept. Baltimore and Ohio in 1920, New Orleans, Texas and Mexico, and Bangor and Aroostook in 1921, financed equipment on the Conditional Sale Basis;

Wheeling and Lake Erie, Minneapolis and St. Louis, and Chicago, Rock Island and Pacific on the Lease Basis in 1921. As railroad credit improved, however, the roads found it possible to finance this equipment on less onerous terms and, while the Service Corporation could adjust its rates and policies to changing market conditions, the stronger roads had no inclination to pool their credit with the weaker. Nor was the Service Corporation more successful in its efforts to achieve pooling of inspection, repair, and rebuilding of equipment and other joint facilities, despite the economies which Mr. Warfield pleaded with the support of Mr. W. W. Colpitts, of the well-known engineering firm of Coverdale and Colpitts. A third project on which the Service Corporation set great hopes was the rebuilding and rehabilitation of existing equipment; it proposed to release cars from the lien of existing mortgages at their depreciated value, subject them to equipment trusts representing the cost of rebuilding, and restore the rebuilt cars (subject to the equipment trust) to the lien of the mortgage, but the mortgage trustees were evidently unwilling to accept such junior liens.

Thus the initial financing appears to have been all that the National Railway Service Corporation accomplished. The original issues were retired by call within a few years, and when the last of the refunding issues were retired in 1935 the Corporation came to a peaceful end.[39]

This experiment has seemed worth reviewing at some

[39] Duncan, *Equipment Obligations,* pp. 82–95, has a good account of National Railway Service Corporation to the end of 1922. For subsequent developments, see chiefly *Moody's.*

length because of suggestions that some pooling or common financing device may be necessary to achieve replacement of obsolete freight cars at a satisfactory rate. Locomotives remain under the owner's control, unless leased on terms satisfactory to the owner, so when more efficient and economical units become available—e.g., the diesel-electric locomotive—individual roads do not hesitate to buy them even at heavy cost, knowing that they will operate the new units themselves and confident that under such circumstances they can pay off the cost from savings in operation. Freight cars, on the other hand, move freely from road to road at a low per diem rental; they may not get back to the owner for months, and will probably spend the greater part of their life on "foreign" lines. One has only to watch almost any freight train to observe how small a proportion of all the cars belong to the particular line over which the train is moving. Under such circumstances there is little incentive for any individual company which is buying new cars to incur the extra cost of roller bearings, or of devices to speed loading and unloading and protect cargo from rough handling; economy dictates the purchase of good standard equipment, meeting interchange standards and rugged enough to avoid excessive repair costs, but without improvements the benefit of which would accrue to other lines most of the time. Only where the nature of the traffic is such as to assure shuttle operation, with no danger of the cars spending time "off-line," can the individual road afford more expensive units, valuable as they might be to shipper or consignee.

Thus the industry struggles along with more rugged but not more economical units, foregoing opportunities to reduce operating costs and cargo damage which not only produces expensive claims but also loses customers. No matter how prompt and generous the settlement, the shipper whose customer has been asked to accept damaged goods, or the consignee who may have been unable to sell or process those goods or to get substitutes in time to avoid losing sales, must be tempted to ship by truck next time. With modern electronic computing and accounting devices, variation in per diem rates to reflect the value of various types of cars should present no overwhelming book-keeping problem, and would seem to be an obvious approach. Failing agreement on that, it might prove possible to work out financing arrangements which would spread the cost of improved equipment over the railroads in general, or at least over a group large enough to reap substantial benefit from the increased investment, but the experience of National Railway Service Corporation points up some of the obstacles.

The leasing plan (of which Equitable Life's is the best-known but not the sole example) has been described briefly above and will be outlined in more detail in Chapter VIII. It has a particular appeal to companies which lack cash for the down payment customary on equipment purchases, or which prefer to save that cash for some other purpose— e.g., Baltimore and Ohio, in connection with the refunding and exchange of debt effected in 1955; to those which for any reason are anxious to avoid showing an increase

## History of Equipment Financing

in funded debt [40] and fixed charges; [41] to those which set little store on ownership of the equipment at the end of the lease period—considering the right of extension at reduced rental adequate in view of the depreciated value of the equipment by that time; and to those anxious to get maximum tax benefits—a phrase which would have been Greek to the rugged individualists of the last century, but which high income tax rates have made a major problem of current finance.

Briefly, the point is that, of every dollar which can be charged to expense, a proportion represented by the company's maximum tax rate—from 87 percent at the highest excess profits rate when that tax was in force to 38 percent in 1949 and 52 percent at present—is absorbed by the resulting reduction in taxes, so that the corporation could truly be said to be spending "13 cent dollars" when in the top excess profit bracket, and "48 cent dollars" at present. Under the leasing plan, since the railroad is not buying the equipment and never becomes its owner, presumably the entire rental can be charged to expense, whereas under conventional financing only interest and depreciation can be so charged, the installments of principal being capital outlays. Since the rental payments cover the entire cost of the equipment within a

[40] Under official accounting, equipment trust certificates and conditional sale contracts both appear on the balance sheet as funded debt, but lease obligations do not.

[41] Rentals are just as fixed a charge as interest would be, but under the official rules are treated as a deduction from operating income rather than an addition to fixed charges, which makes a difference in figuring certain ratios.

fifteen-year period, this is equivalent to 6⅔ percent a year, as compared with depreciation charges averaging in 1955 around 4.5 percent on locomotives (other than steam locomotives) and 3.15 percent on the freight car investment of Class I railroads; only 5 percent of the locomotive investment carried depreciation at 5 percent or more, and only one half of one percent of the freight car investment at 4 percent or more.[42] Thus, under the lease plan, the charge against taxable income appears to be fully two percentage points higher than the depreciation on locomotive and three points higher than that on freight cars; if the railroad can reimburse itself for half [43] this difference from tax savings, over the term of the lease this represents a sum which it may well consider adequate compensation for not owning the fifteen-year old units at termination of the lease, particularly in view of the greatly reduced rental at which it can obtain use of the equipment under the renewal option.

The latest development in the field is the plan (outlined in more detail in Chapter VIII) which was recently presented by Mr. James M. Symes, president of the Pennsylvania Railroad, for a government-financed corporation to buy rolling stock for lease to the railroads, claiming that

[42] *Statistics of Railways* (1955), Table 97. The rate at which depreciation is allowed for income tax purposes may exceed the figure shown in Interstate Commerce Commission reports when "accelerated depreciation" is involved. This may be amortization of defense projects (see page 3 above) or may take one of the optional forms authorized by the Revenue Act of 1954 (Section 167), substituting "diminishing balance" or "sum of the digits" calculations for straight-line depreciation.

[43] More than half, when the tax rate exceeds 50 percent.

## History of Equipment Financing

in no other way can they obtain the equipment needed at prices which they can afford to pay.[44]

[44] See the New York *Times,* July 25, 1957; The New York *Herald-Tribune* and the *Wall Street Journal,* same date; *Railway Age,* July 29, 1957; particularly *Traffic World,* July 27, 1957.

*CHAPTER IV*

# Legal Status of Equipment Obligations

DUNCAN [1] has a chapter, "Equipment Obligations at Common Law," citing more than a hundred cases which to the layman seem quite confusing and of purely historical interest. His conclusion is:

> Equipment contracts of conditional sale and lease do not pass title until the contract is fulfilled. . . . it is now [2] immaterial whether the sale agreement be drawn as a conditional sale or as a bailment with an option to purchase in the bailee. Courts have shown a decided tendency to interpret all so-called leases, even though properly drawn, as possessing no greater validity than conditional sales. Great care in drawing up the agreement and in formulating its terms is necessary to avoid the possibility of having a court interpret the contract as a completed sale with a mortgage lien back. Title must be expressly reserved to the conditional seller or lessor, and there must be no ambiguity in the contract on this point. Delivery of the equipment should not precede the making of the agreement, nor should any circumstances be permitted to arise by which prior title can be construed to have been in the railroad company. The sale or lease must be bona fide,

---

[1] Kenneth Duncan, *Equipment Obligations* (New York, Appleton, 1924), pp. 97–154.

[2] I.e., with conditional sales authorized by statute in all states.

## Legal Status

there must be no doubt as to the right of the seller to give title, and there must be no taint or suspicion of fraud.

Equipment trust funds should never be used for any other purpose than for the acquisition of the equipment and should be kept quite distinct from any other funds of the obligor corporation. . . .

Where statutory provisions for recording of contracts, marking of equipment, and other legal requirements exist, noncompliance with such provisions is fatal. . . .

If faithful attention has been given to these incidents of the law, there is no question but that railroad equipment contracts are of unimpeachable legality, and that the lien of the equipment creditor will be superior to that of any other creditors of the obligor railroad company, whether they be purchasers for value with or without notice, judgment creditors, mortgagees of the railroad company, holders of receivers' certificates, or any other lienors whatever.[3]

Smith expresses the same conclusion:

Conditional sales of railroad equipment as well as of other property are recognized everywhere. As long as it is a conditional sale and not a chattel mortgage, the holder of the equipment obligation is secure. . . .

In general, by 1900 the rights of holders of equipment obligations had been clearly enough defined by the courts as to grant them a virtually impregnable position, subject only to having contracts drawn in terms which did not constitute chattel mortgages and absent any *fraudulent* avoidance of the rights of mortgage bondholders.[4]

Duncan goes on to say:

[3] Duncan, *Equipment Obligations,* pp. 146–48.

[4] Paul Smith, Jr., The Development of the Legal Status of American Railroad Equipment Securities (unpublished J.S.D. dissertation, School of Law, New York University, 1950), pp. 28, 35.

*Legal Status*

In every state of the Union, as well as in the territory of Alaska, laws affirming the legality and regulating conditional sales of railroad equipment and rolling stock have been enacted . . . four important parts, or main provisions, . . . appear in nearly all of the acts. . . .

The first part of the act contains a declaration that conditional sales or leases of railway rolling stock and equipment shall be legal. The second part declares that such agreements shall be invalid both at law and in equity as against creditors of the vendee and subsequent bona fide purchasers for value without notice, unless (a) the said contracts be in writing and be properly acknowledged or proved, (b) the said contracts are filed for record as directed in the statute, and (c) the locomotives and/or cars covered by the agreement are marked with the name of the owner or lessor. The third part describes in detail the procedure of recording. . . . The fourth part provides that the effect of the act shall not be to invalidate any prior agreements already in force.[5]

These state statutes will be of purely historical interest in another decade, as recent agreements have been, and as future ones presumably will be, recorded under Section 20c added to the Interstate Commerce Act in 1952.

Any mortgage, lease, equipment trust agreement, conditional sale agreement, or other instrument evidencing the mortgage, lease, conditional sale, or bailment of railroad cars, locomotives, or other rolling stock, used or intended for use in connection with interstate commerce, or any assignment of rights or interest under any such instrument, or any supplement or amendment to any such instrument or assignment (including any release, discharge or satisfaction thereof, in whole or in part), may be filed with the Commission, provided such instru-

---

[5] Duncan, *Equipment Obligations*, pp. 155, 157.

## Legal Status

ment, assignment, supplement, or amendment is in writing, executed by the parties thereto, and acknowledged or verified in accordance with such requirements as the Commission shall prescribe; and any such instrument or other document, when so filed with the Commission, shall constitute notice to and shall be valid and enforceable against all persons including, without limitation, any purchaser from, or mortgagee, creditor, receiver, or trustee in bankruptcy of, the mortgagor, buyer, lessee or bailee of the equipment covered thereby, from and after the time such instrument or other document is so filed with the Commission; and such instrument or other document need not be otherwise filed, deposited, registered or recorded under the provisions of any other law of the United States of America, or of any State (or political subdivision thereof), territory, district or possession thereof, respecting the filing, deposit, registration or recordation of such instruments or documents. The Commission shall establish and maintain a system for the recordation of each such instrument or document, filed pursuant to the provisions of this section, and shall cause to be marked or stamped thereon, a consecutive number, as well as the date and hour of such recordation, and shall maintain, open to public inspection, an index of all such instruments or documents, including any assignment, amendment, release, discharge or satisfaction thereof, and shall record, in such index the names and addresses of the principal debtors, trustees, guarantors and other parties thereto, as well as such other facts as may be necessary to facilitate the determination of the rights of the parties to such transaction.[6]

The new statute is at once less burdensome and more effective than the old. One recording covers the entire country, whereas a dozen or more might be necessary under the state acts: it has been customary to record in

---
[6] 66 *Stat.* 724.

each jurisdiction in which the road operates and, if the equipment is delivered "off-line," then also in the states through which it must pass on the way to the purchaser. Moreover nothing short of recording in 48 states would give complete protection in the case of freight cars, which may move across the continent in interchange service. It was generally felt that the value of an individual freight car was not sufficiently great, and the possibility of any considerable number being available for attachment by creditors in an unprotected spot was too small, to constitute a serious risk, but the federal statute obviously offers better protection.

It likewise eliminates the requirement for marking the equipment, although lenders and lessors have generally continued to stipulate such marking. Marking no doubt has a salutary moral effect, assuring all concerned that in the face of a metal plate bearing in letters an inch high some such legend as "Guaranty Trust Company of New York, trustee, owner" no one can claim to be an innocent purchaser or deceived creditor, that no court can make trouble by holding such notice necessary (on the basis of established custom) despite the absence of any such stipulation in the statute, and that no present or future buyer of the certificates will be disturbed by absence of the familiar provision. Securities must be not only valid but salable; to change a well-established practice, the buyer as well as the lawyer must be satisfied.

The most important development within this century in the status of equipment obligations, however, was the Rock Island controversy and the legislation which grew

## Legal Status

out of it. On June 7, 1933, Chicago, Rock Island and Pacific Railway Company filed a petition for reorganization under Section 77 of the Bankruptcy Act, enacted earlier in the year with a view to simplifying, expediting, and improving railroad reorganization procedure,[7] hitherto effected through equity receiverships. One of the provisions of that act permits the court to "enjoin or stay the commencement or continuance of any judicial proceeding to enforce any lien upon the estate [i.e., the property of the debtor] until after the final decree." Under that authority, and on the urging of mortgage bondholders who argued that equipment covered by the equipment trusts was "property of the debtor" within the meaning of Section 77,[8] the court on December 28, 1933, ordered the Bankruptcy Trustees to "make no further payment on account of rentals; principal; interest; or dividends due, or to become due, under any of the . . . Equipment Trust Agreements of the debtor."[9]

In the words of Mr. Carroll Shanks, speaking before the Association of Life Insurance Counsel on December 3, 1935:

It was contended that equipment trust holders were in the same position as mortgage bondholders, that they were all

[7] 47 *Stat.* 1474.

[8] "In this Rock Island matter, we were met by a suggestion . . . that in railroad bankruptcy proceedings these equipments were nothing more than chattel mortgages and should be scaled down." Testimony of General Counsel of the Rock Island System, *Hearings before Committee on the Judiciary on H.R. 6249,* 74th Cong., 1st Session 268 (1935), as quoted by Smith.

[9] *In re* Chicago, Rock Island and Pacific Railway, N.D. Ill. Dec. 28, 1933, as quoted by Smith.

bound in pending the preparation of a plan, and that equipment trust holders should have no more right to take their equipment than the mortgage bondholders should have to foreclose upon their property. To further this contention, it was said that equipment trust holders had merely a lien upon the property, that the title retained in the trustee . . . was merely a security title, in other words, a mortgage.[10]

Certificate holders, naturally, did not agree with this contention, but faced the prospect of long and dubious litigation (especially after the Supreme Court had upheld an order enjoining certain secured creditors from selling their collateral)[11] until Congress resolved the matter by a clarifying amendment to Section 77, adding in subsection (j) the following sentence:

The title of any owner, whether as trustee or otherwise, to rolling-stock equipment leased or conditionally sold to the debtor, and any right of such owner to take possession of such property in compliance with the provisions of any such lease or conditional sale contract, shall not be affected by the provisions of this section.[12]

Smith points out that the obvious effect of the amendment was to make railroad equipment the single important exception to the rule that reorganization courts may, at least temporarily, restrain conditional vendors from repossessing their equipment, pointing out contrary cases dealing with other types of equipment.[13]

[10] Smith, Development of Legal Status, p. 49.
[11] Continental Illinois National Bank and Trust Company v. Chicago, Rock Island and Pacific Railway, 294 U.S. 648 (1935), as quoted by Smith.
[12] 49 *Stat.* 911.
[13] *In re* Lake's Laundry, Inc., 79 2d 326 (2d Cir. 1935), *cert. denied*, 296 U.S. 622; *In re* Pointer Brewing Co., 105 F2d 478 (8th Cir.

## Legal Status

Fortified by subsection (j), the committee representing the holders of equipment trust certificates was able to conclude with the bankruptcy trustees the satisfactory settlement outlined in the next chapter, and the representatives of most other equipment issues were equally successful.

A similar but not identical provision appears in Section 20b of the Interstate Commerce Act dealing with "voluntary" modification of the rights of security holders —the so-called Mahaffie Act.

Provided, That the provisions of this section shall not apply to any equipment trust certificates in respect of which a carrier is obligated, or to any evidences of indebtedness of a carrier the payment of which is secured in any manner solely by equipment, or to any instrument, whether an agreement, lease, conditional-sale agreement or otherwise, pursuant to which such equipment trust certificates or such evidences of indebtedness shall have been issued or by which they are secured.[14]

1939); *In re* White Plains Ice Service, Inc., 109 F2d 913 (2d Cir. 1940); *In re* Ideal Laundry 10 F Supp. 719 (N.D. Calif. 1935).

However, Public Law 85-295, approved September 4, 1957, in effect extended this exception to aircraft and aircraft equipment of air carriers in the following language:

"(5) Notwithstanding any other provisions of Chapter X [of the Bankruptcy Act], the title of any owner, whether as trustee or otherwise, to aircraft, aircraft engines, propellers, appliances and spare parts (as any of such are defined in the Civil Aeronautics Act of 1938, as now in effect or hereafter amended) leased, subleased or conditionally sold to any air carrier which is operating pursuant to a certificate of convenience and necessity issued by the Civil Aeronautics Board, and any right of such owner or of any other lessor to such air carrier to take possession of such property in compliance with the provisions of any such lease or conditional sale contract shall not be affected by the provisions of Chapter X if the terms of such lease or conditional sale so provide."

[14] 62 *Stat.* 162.

This, incidentally, would appear to include chattel mortgages secured *solely* by equipment, but investors cannot be expected to warm up those as long as the exception in Section 77 is limited to "equipment leased or conditionally sold."

The chief subsequent development in the legal status of equipment obligations turns upon recent unsuccessful attempts to prevent Reconstruction Finance Corporation from exercising its rights as holder of equipment trust certificates in the New York, Ontario and Western reorganization. That road, extending from Weehawken on the Hudson River to Oswego on Lake Ontario, began proceedings in 1937 for reorganization under Section 77 of the Bankruptcy Act. No plan of reorganization was ever approved, the reorganization proceedings eventually being abandoned as hopeless. Receivers were appointed in January, 1957, operation stopped on March 29, and the properties sold piecemeal in June, 1957.[15]

Meanwhile, however, the trustees in bankruptcy, under authorization of the court, had sold ten-year serial equipment trust certificates to the Reconstruction Finance Corporation in 1945 and again in 1947 to provide funds for the purchase of diesel-electric locomotives. The trustees maintained the stipulated 3 percent interest payments, but defaulted the quarterly installments of principal in the summer of 1949. Negotiations with the RFC for refinancing the matured certificates were unsuccessful; in fact the trustees failed to maintain even the reduced schedule

[15] See the New York *Times,* January 13, 1957; March 30, 1957; and June 28, 1957.

## Legal Status

of principal payments contemplated under the refinancing proposals. On May 14, 1953, the RFC sent the surviving bankruptcy trustee (one having died) a notice rescinding its previous approval of the proposed refinancing, and on July 1, 1953, requested The Hanover Bank, as trustee of the equipment issues, to proceed with steps for the protection and enforcement of its rights as holder of the certificates. The equipment trustee thereupon declared the principal of both issues to be due and payable immediately, and filed a petition for leave to enforce its rights and remedies under the equipment trusts, repossessing and selling the locomotives and obtaining a judgment for any deficiency.

At a hearing on July 29 the bankruptcy trustee and various other parties requested time in which to negotiate further with the RFC, and over the strenuous objection of the equipment trustee the District Court adjourned the hearing for 90 days. During the period of adjournment an agreement was reached that, upon entry by the District Court of an order granting the equipment trustee authority to proceed, the latter would be instructed by RFC not to proceed before June 29, 1954, provided the bankruptcy trustee should maintain during that period the payments specified in the new agreement, somewhat less than those required under the original trusts. This agreement was approved by the District Court, but appealed by two bondholders, on the basis that it in effect authorized the abandonment of operations—on termination of the agreement June 29, 1954, or on earlier default —and therefore required the approval of the Interstate

Commerce Commission, citing as "decisive of this appeal" the United States Supreme Court decision in Smith v. Hoboken R. Co., 328 U.S. 123 (1946), holding that the bankruptcy court could not without such approval permit the owner of a leased line to terminate the lease and reenter his property.

The Circuit Court of Appeals rejected this appeal,[16] saying:

We think the *Smith* decision inapposite here. In the first place, the provisions of Section 77(b) [17] have no application to the orders now before us. For, by an amendment enacted in 1935, Congress added to Section 77(j) this sentence: "The title of any owner, whether as trustee or otherwise, to rolling-stock equipment leased or conditionally sold to the debtor, and any right of such owner to take possession of such property in compliance with the provisions of any such lease or conditional sale contract, shall not be affected by the provisions of this section."

The legislative history shows that Congress, recognizing the substantial benefits to railroads which result from such equipment-agreements, desired to remove any possible doubt— stemming in part from *Continental Illinois National Bank & Trust Co.* v. *Chicago, Rock Island and Pacific Ry Co.*, 294 U.S. 648—as to the ability of owners of equipment trust certificates promptly, on default, to repossess the equipment, despite the pendency of bankruptcy-reorganization proceedings. . . . we think that the words "this section" refers to Section 77 as a whole and not merely to paragraph (j).

[16] 215 F2d 63, pp. 63–69 (1954).

[17] "Under Section 77(b) of the Bankruptcy Act [11 U.S.C. Section 205(b)], a plan of reorganization, which must be formulated by the Interstate Commerce Commission, can modify or alter the rights of creditors of the debtor-railroad and can cure or waive defaults of the debtor under a lease." *Ibid.*, p. 67.

## Legal Status

Moreover, significantly unlike the fact of the *Smith* case, here The Hanover Bank sought to enforce contracts executed, by the bankruptcy trustee, after the bankruptcy and by the express authority of the bankruptcy-reorganization court. Whether the *Smith*-case doctrine would govern the lease of a railroad line similarly executed, we need not now decide. But we think that doctrine cannot apply to equipment-trust obligations which the bankruptcy court has authorized.

Nor, all else aside, is 49 U.S.C. Section 1 (18) [18] relevant here. . . . No Commission approval is necessary where the cessation of operations results, not from the volition of the railroad or its bankruptcy-trustee, but from the exercise of the supervening rights, here recognized by the Bankruptcy Act, of third persons. . . . Especially in a case like this, if such approval were required before equipment-trust certificate-holders could recapture the equipment on default, the market for such certificates might well dry up, and accordingly railroad reorganization trustees might often be unable to procure needed equipment, with the consequence that suspension of operations would often be accelerated rather than avoided.[19]

Thus the decision, which was not appealed, fully sustained the position of the equipment trustee, although it would obviously have been even more valuable in defining the status of equipment obligations in general if it had not involved the additional fact that the agreements in question were obligations of the bankruptcy trustee rather than of the bankrupt railroad. (For eventual sale of the

---

[18] This section reads, in part, as follows: "No carrier by railroad . . . shall abandon all or any portion of a line of railroad, or the operation thereof, unless and until there shall first have been obtained from the Commission a certificate that the present or future public convenience and necessity permit of such abandonment."

[19] 215 F2d 63, pp. 68–69.

locomotives and application of the proceeds, see Chapter V.)

Both statutes and cases, then, confirm the right of the equipment creditor to repossess his rolling stock if the bankruptcy trustee does not make the payments specified in the agreement. The trustee may "adopt" the agreement—i.e., undertake all specified payments, principal and interest, thereby preserving all rights to the use, and ultimate ownership, of the equipment involved; he may "reject" the agreement, thereby terminating his liability save for the reasonable rental value of the equipment (not necessarily the rental specified in the agreement) up to the time of its surrender to the equipment creditors; or he may, if the equipment creditors do not insist upon an immediate choice, neither adopt nor reject, continuing to use the equipment and incur liability for its reasonable rental value,[20] without prejudice to the right of the equipment creditors to repossess if and when they decide to invoke that remedy.

[20] Thomas v. Western Car Co., 149 U.S. 95 (1893); Kneeland v. American Loan & Trust Co., 136 U.S. 89 (1890); Platt v. Philadelphia & R.R.R., 84 Fed. 535 (3d Cir. 1898); New York Trust Co. v. Kenan, Equity No. 884-J, S.D. Fla. Nov. 8, 1943; Turner v. Indianapolis, B. & W. Ry., 24 Fed. Cas. 372, No. 14, 260 (C.C.D. Ind. 1879); Lane v. Macon & A. Ry., 96 Ga. 630, 24 S.E. 157 (1895); see Note, Compensation to Trustee for Use of Railroad Equipment under Disaffirmed Lease, 49 Yale L.J. 1483 (1940)—all as cited by Smith, Development of Legal Status, p. 36.

But the trustee is not liable for the rental prior to his appointment (Smith, p. 37, citing the first two of the cases above); that remains simply the obligation of the debtor corporation, unless and until the trustee "adopts" the agreement.

## Legal Status

In actual practice this third course is likely to be followed for some months. If the value and necessity of the equipment are such that the road cannot do without it and the creditors have no doubt that repossession would be profitable, the trustee may (but will not necessarily) "adopt" promptly; if the equipment is clearly not necessary and useful he can be expected to "reject" promptly; if the equipment is useful but perhaps not essential, and the equipment creditors are hesitant about the expense and risks of repossession (as may well be the case when traffic is light and demand for equipment low), the bankruptcy trustee will probably stall along trying to reach some compromise settlement—especially if other creditors are litigating the right of repossession; the ingenuity of attorneys can be expected to supply new arguments for such litigation in spite of statutes and precedents. Thus the opening months of the reorganization proceeding may be devoted to sparring between the equipment creditors, the other creditors, and the bankruptcy trustee, as each seeks to determine the strength of its position and the best bargain it can safely work out. In the end, payments on those equipment obligations which are adequately secured will probably be maintained without formal "adoption" of the agreement by the trustee; the equipment creditors will be satisfied with such payments because, being at a rate exceeding depreciation on the equipment, each payment strengthens the position of the outstanding balance, and formal "adoption" of the agreement will be made only by the reorganized company, which by the decree ending the proceedings will be directed to assume the agreement as to any installments not retired during the reorganization.

In addition to the all-important statutes bearing upon the position of equipment obligations in receivership or reorganization proceedings, there are others which concern them directly or indirectly. Section 10 of the Clayton Act [21] contains a prohibition against dealings in securities otherwise than by competitive bidding, where an interlocking directorate exists between carrier and purchaser, and the first competitive bidding rules were issued by the Interstate Commerce Commission under this authority, effective January 1, 1920.[22]

The fundamental statute governing the marketing of equipment obligations is Section 20a,[23] added to the Interstate Commerce Act by the Transportation Act of 1920.[24] Paragraph (2) of that section makes it

unlawful for any carrier to issue . . . any bond or other evidence of interest in or indebtedness of the carrier (hereinafter in this section collectively termed "securities") or to assume any obligation or liability as lessor, lessee, guarantor, indorser, surety or otherwise, in respect of the securities of any other person . . . unless and until . . . the commission by order authorizes such issue or assumption.

Paragraph (4) gives the commission power to prescribe the form and content of applications for such authorization; paragraph (11) makes any security issued without

[21] 38 *Stat.* 734 (1941); 15 U.S.C. Section 20 (1952).
[22] 56 I.C.C. 847 (1920).     [23] 49 U.S.C. 20a (1952).
[24] 41 *Stat.* 456.

## Legal Status

the required authorization void, and provides appropriate civil and criminal penalties; paragraph (6) provides for notice to governors of states in which the carrier operates, and an opportunity for state authorities to make such representations as they may deem just and proper; and paragraph (7) specifies:

The jurisdiction conferred upon the commission by this section shall be exclusive and plenary, and a carrier may issue securities and assume obligations or liabilities in accordance with the provisions of this section without securing approval other than as specified herein.

Thus Section 20a specifically puts the Interstate Commerce Commission in charge of railroad financing, and supersedes the statutes by which various states [25] had previously regulated the issue of securities by carriers within their respective jurisdictions.

The form and contents of applications for authority to issue securities under Section 20a, including evidence of corporate authority and appropriate corporate action, of the legality and necessity of the proposal, of its object, of the finances of the railroad, of the equipment involved (its cost, the manner of its purchase, and the reason for accepting the particular bid if not the lowest received), and of all contracts or underwritings in con-

[25] Fifteen in all, according to Smith, Development of Legal Status, p. 54, who cites as his authorities Wm. Zebina Ripley, *Railroads: Finance and Organization* (New York, Longmans, Green & Co., 1915), p. 286, and David Philip Locklin, *Regulation of Security Issues by the Interstate Commerce Commission* (Urbana, Ill., University of Illinois, 1925), pp. 20–21.

nection with the proposed sale, including price, rate, and expenses, are prescribed by the rules and regulations of the commission.[26] The commission indicated its preference for competitive bidding in the sale of equipment trust certificates as early as 1924,[27] but continued for a few years to permit sales by private negotiation, over the objections of Commissioner Eastman.[28]

There was clearly some doubt within the commission as to its authority to require competitive bidding. In the Union Pacific case, while urging "that the carriers should give serious thought to the marketing of these, and perhaps other securities, on a competitive basis," the opinion also says, "It is not our present purpose and perhaps not our function to require the observance of any particular method in railway financing." In the New York Central case, Commissioner Eastman himself says:

I should be in favor of requiring competitive bidding without any other alternative, except that I doubt our power to do this. We have power to fix a reasonable minimum price and, if our conclusion as to such price is questioned, I believe that we also have power to require the matter to be determined by the practical test of competitive bidding.

In another case in the same year, Commissioner Woodlock says: "It seems very doubtful . . . that the law gives us power to prescribe so-called 'competitive bidding' for

[26] 49 Code Fed. Regs. Section 56.1–3 (Supp. 1957).
[27] Union Pacific Equipment Trust, Series D, 86 I.C.C. 612, 614 (1924).
[28] New York Central Lines Equipment Trust of 1925, 99 I.C.C. 121, 124 (1925); Northern Pacific Equipment Trust of 1925, 99 I.C.C. 164, 165 (1925); Pennsylvania Railroad General Equipment Trust, Series D, 111 I.C.C. 241, 244 (1926).

## Legal Status

railroad securities." [29] In the Pennsylvania case Eastman repeats the recommendation for requiring competitive bidding if the applicant is unwilling to accept the commission's determination of price, observing: "Some contend that we are without power to pursue this course, but I know of no better way of finding out than by putting it to the test."

In June, 1926, in its opinion on *Western Maryland Equipment Trust Series D*,[30] which had been successfully sold by competitive bidding, the commission indicated its intention of requiring future sales to be by competitive bidding under the procedure previously prescribed in connection with the Clayton Act.[31] Later in the year it allowed other roads to negotiate sales with underwriters of their own selection, on the condition that the latter improve their bids to figures matching those realized on recent competitive sales.[32] A couple of years later, however, a carrier which had received unsatisfactory bids on its invitations for competitive bidding and sought authority for a negotiated sale on better terms, was required to readvertise and try again, with the alternative of temporary financing if necessary until the market should improve, the commission observing: "We can hardly expect banks to continue to submit tenders for equipment obligations on invitation from carriers if the carriers may reject all bids

---

[29] Chicago, Milwaukee and St. Paul Equipment Trust, 99 I.C.C. 682, 689. Detailed references to the other cases are given in footnotes immediately preceding.

[30] 111 I.C.C. 434 (1926).    [31] 56 I.C.C. 847 (1920).

[32] Chicago, St. M. and O. Equipment Trust, 117 I.C.C. 11 (1926); Illinois Central Equipment Trust, 117 I.C.C. 15 (1926).

and after thus testing the investment market place the obligations privately." [33] There appears to be no subsequent case in which the commission has permitted the sale of equipment trust certificates without competitive bidding.

The commission early decided that a conditional sale contract, which accomplishes the same purpose as an equipment trust agreement, is not in itself a security or other evidence of indebtedness within the meaning of Section 20a, dismissing as beyond its jurisdiction an application for authority to purchase a locomotive under such a contract.[34] In several subsequent cases, which involved notes or certificates secured by conditional sale contracts or lease, the commission limited its approval to the notes or certificates, repeating that the underlying contract or lease did not constitute an issue of securities or require its consent.[35]

The matter was a little confused, however, by an early case [36] in which the commission did authorize (perhaps by inadvertence, since neither party raised the point) an equipment lease securing deferred payments for which no notes or other securities were to be issued, and by a later decision holding that a contract providing for deferred payments on real estate "constitutes evidence of in-

[33] Chicago, St. P., M. and O. Ry. Co. Equipment Trust, 145 I.C.C. 444 (1928).

[34] Purchase-Contract Application of La. Ry. and Nav. Co., 67 I.C.C. 808 (1921).

[35] Notes of Lake Erie, Franklin and Clarion R.R., 99 I.C.C. 404 (1925); Norfolk S.R.R. Co., Receivers' Notes, 207 I.C.C. 121 (1935); Chicago and E.I. Ry. Co. Trustees' Equipment-Trust Certificates, 217 I.C.C. 439 (1936).

[36] Equipment Lease of Illinois Central R.R., 71 I.C.C. 406 (1922).

## Legal Status

debtedness of applicant and is within the definition of 'securities' included in Section 20a (2)," though no notes or other securities to cover the deferred payments were to be issued.[37]

Accordingly a test case [38] was brought before the full commission, the previous decisions having been by Division 4 (finance) or Division 5 (motor carriers). Lehigh Valley applied for authority to execute a conditional sale contract with Bethlehem Steel Company for the purchase of cars, and then filed a motion to dismiss the application for want of jurisdiction. The commission, after discussing the statute and various rules of construction at some length, and citing various court cases and its own prior rulings, including those mentioned above, came to the conclusions that

the provisions [of Section 20a] were intended to apply to obligations negotiable or quasi-negotiable in character, such as are issued for the purpose of railroad financing. . . . The agreement in question has none of the attributes of negotiability, and will not be issued or uttered, but merely executed and delivered. So far as the applicant is concerned, no proceeds will be realized therefrom . . . the contract . . . under consideration . . . is not a security within the meaning of Section 20a, and . . . we have no jurisdiction over its execution.

This decision was a landmark, the commission remarking a few years later in *Chicago, B. and Q.R. Co. Notes* [39] that

---
[37] Washington Motor Coach Co., Inc.—Stock, 5 M.C.C. 524 (1938).
[38] Lehigh Valley R. Co. Conditional Sale Contract, 233 I.C.C. 359 (1939).
[39] 254 I.C.C. 175 (1943).

Thereafter many railroads . . . purchased a large number of units of equipment, the cost of which amounted to a very substantial sum, under conditional sale contracts and lease agreements. By these methods the railroads in many instances avoided the making of initial cash payments. . . .

They also avoided our scrutiny of the reasonableness of the prices to be paid for the equipment, the offering of securities . . . for sale through competitive bidding, and our approval of the selling price.

The commission authorized the issuance of promissory notes as additional security for conditional sale contracts entered into between 1937 and 1941, in order that the railroad might include the contract indebtedness in its computation of invested capital under the excess-profits tax, but warned the railroads against expecting authority to issue notes against future conditional sale contracts and "assumed that hereafter railroads will, in most instances, finance the acquisition of equipment through equipment trust agreements and leases rather than through conditional sale contracts."

This assumption has conspicuously not been realized. From approximately $34,000,000 in 1942, the first year in which it was separately reported, such financing increased to a peak of $413,000,000 in 1951, followed by $347,000,000 in 1952, and a total of $400,000,000 in 1953–55.[40] Accordingly the commission recommended in its annual report for 1952

that Section 20a (2) requiring authorization by the Commission of the issuance of securities by certain common carriers and other corporations, be amended by including any contract

[40] *Statistics of Railways,* Tables 148 and 146-A.

## Legal Status

for the purchase or lease of equipment not to be fully performed within one year from the date of the contract.[41]

This recommendation was repeated in three subsequent reports, without result.

Since this recommendation covers leases as well as purchase agreements, it would of course include the Equitable and other lease plans.[42] Another recommendation, specifically aimed at those plans is

that Section 1 (15) be amended so as to authorize the Commission thereunder to determine the compensation to be paid and the terms of any other contract, agreement or arrangement for the use of any locomotive, car or other vehicle not owned by the carrier using it (and whether or not owned by another carrier).[43]

This recommendation was likewise repeated in three subsequent reports, without action.

Neither recommendation appeared in the 1956 report, the commission saying: "A number of recommendations which were repeated for many years in the past have been omitted because they pertained to less urgent matters. We feel that a busy Congress should have the benefit of selectivity in this respect." [44]

In the absence of Interstate Commerce Commission action on the issuance of conditional sale contracts, the Public Service Commission of New York has asserted

[41] Interstate Commerce Commission, 66th Annual Report (1952), p. 147.
[42] See below, Chapter VIII.
[43] Interstate Commerce Commission, 66th Annual Report (1952), p. 147.
[44] I.C.C., 70th Annual Report (1956), p. 159.

jurisdiction over such issues where railroads in the state are concerned. Delaware and Hudson obtained authorization from the Public Service Commission for a $15,800,000 conditional sale contract in 1952,[45] and New York Central filed under protest in connection with a $21,000,000 diesel locomotive purchase in the following year, stating:

> the applicant does not admit that the Commission approval or authorization of . . . the Conditional Sale Agreement is required by law . . . in . . . counsel's opinion the financing of equipment purchases . . . by railroads engaged in interstate commerce . . . lies in a field which has been occupied by the Federal Government . . . to the exclusion of . . . any State regulatory bodies . . . any fee which applicant may be required to pay . . . will constitute an undue burden on interstate commerce. Moreover, applicant points out that this case is distinguishable from the Delaware & Hudson case, in that applicant, unlike the Delaware & Hudson, is a consolidated railroad corporation of New York and five other States.[46]

These protests were over-ruled [47] on the basis of *County Transportation*,[48] and the Public Service Commission appears to be in the saddle unless the railroad should take a successful appeal to the courts.

This precedent may or may not be followed in other

---

[45] Case #15,719 decided April 16, 1952 and reported at p. 351 of Annual Report 1952, vol. 1. This, incidentally, gives an excellent statement of the railroad's reason for this financing.

[46] As quoted by John Stevenson, "Financing of Railroad Equipment," *The Analysts Journal,* IX (No. 5, November, 1953), 14.

[47] Case #16,369; orders August 18, 1953, and January 14, 1954, mentioned briefly in Public Service Commission Annual Report 1955, I, 241.

[48] 303 N.Y. 391 (1952).

## Legal Status

states. I am informed that Illinois required authorization insofar as the transaction concerned a subsidiary within that state, but is marking time as far as New York Central generally is concerned, while Michigan and Ohio have indicated interest only in such local items as signal equipment, in effect disclaiming jurisdiction over the purchase of rolling stock. Obviously the action of each state will reflect the philosophy and make-up of its regulatory authorities, the statutes under which they operate, and the precedents there and elsewhere.

The Securities Act of 1933, after defining "securities" in the broadest terms, defines the term "issuer" to mean "every person who issues or proposes to issue any security; . . . except that with respect to equipment trust certificates or like securities, the term 'issuer' means the person by whom the equipment or property is or is to be used . . . ," and then proceeds to exempt "(6) Any security issued by a common or contract carrier issuance of which is subject to the provisions of Section 20a of Title 49." [49] Thus the Securities Act presents no problem for railroad equipment trust certificates, but issues which have not been authorized by the Interstate Commerce Commission under Section 20a, such as conditional sale contracts or the obligations of noncarrier corporations, can obtain exemption only under the provision of Section 77d(1) covering "transactions by an issuer not involving any public offering."

Another class of statutes bearing on equipment obligations includes those defining their status as legal invest-

[49] 48 *Stat.* 74 (1933); 15 U.S.C. Section 77b (4) and (6) respectively.

ments for banks and/or insurance companies. Smith [50] lists some seventeen states having such statutes, of which New York is obviously the most important, having about half the savings bank deposits of the country and a similar proportion of life insurance assets. Section 235 of the Banking Law, governing the investment of savings bank funds, includes in paragraph 7(3)c "equipment trust obligations comprising bonds, notes and certificates" covering "new standard-gauge rolling stock," subject to certain stipulations as to size, earnings, and financial record of the railroad, a down payment of at least twenty percent, and approximately equal annual or semiannual maturities over a period not exceeding fifteen years. The Insurance Law, in Section 81(4)b, authorizes life insurance companies to invest in

Equipment trust obligations or certificates which are adequately secured or other adequately secured instruments evidencing an interest in transportation equipment wholly or in part within the United States and a right to receive determined portions of rental, purchase or other fixed obligatory payments for the use or purchase of such property.

Thus the two statutes stand at opposite poles, the one specifying merely the type and adequacy of the security, while the other endeavors to spell out all the details; they may be considered representative of the full range within which the various statutes may lie.

[50] Development of Legal Status, p. 91, footnote 183.

*CHAPTER V*

# Experience in Receivership and Reorganization [1]

IT is sometimes assumed that equipment obligations are riskless investments. The record does not bear this out, but it does show many cases in which payment on such obligations has been maintained right through receivership or reorganization proceedings, others in which the delays involved have been minor, and almost none involving any substantial loss for the holder able and willing to await the outcome.

Dewing, writing in 1934, describes the Denver and Rio Grande reorganization of 1886 as "the only instance in the history of American railway finance where the holders of equipment obligations issued under the Philadelphia Plan were forced to suffer for a considerable period." [2]

[1] Railroad reorganizations were effected through equity receiverships until the addition of Section 77 to the Bankruptcy Act in 1933; since that time most reorganization proceedings have been under Section 77. Consequently the court officers in charge of the properties were receivers in the earlier proceedings, bankruptcy trustees in most of the later. In raising funds, on the authority of the court, these officers borrow on receivers' certificates or trustees' certificates, the security for which is specified by the order authorizing their issuance.

[2] Arthur Stone Dewing, *A Study of Corporation Securities* (New York, The Ronald Press Company, 1934), p. 371, footnote ww, from which the following account is taken.

The Denver, a narrow gauge railroad built in the seventies to capitalize the civic pride of Denver (by-passed by the Union Pacific) and the optimism of the time, failed in the depression of 1884. It had outstanding, in addition to a small issue of first mortgage bonds and large issues of junior bonds and stock, some $3,500,000 6 percent and 7 percent equipment trust certificates. The equipment, besides being narrow gauge—which both eliminated most potential purchasers and increased the expense of any delivery—was worn, dilapidated, and out of repair. Experts advised buying other equipment at currently depressed prices, if the equipment creditors should refuse to compromise their claim. Consequently, the other creditors rejected a plan which proposed refunding the equipment obligations into first mortgage bonds, and the equipment creditors, fearing that repossession might prove disastrous, eventually accepted a plan which provided 17 percent in cash and 120 percent in consolidated (junior) mortgage bonds for the equipment certificates, together with new noncumulative preferred stock in the amount of 20 percent for the 6 percent certificates and 30 percent for the 7 percent series. Ultimately the new securities proved salable for enough to get the holders out without loss.

Among the roads which failed in the next depression, about ten years later, was the Norfolk and Western, which connects the coal fields of West Virginia with the port of Norfolk. Dewing [3] says that the reorganization of 1896,

[3] *Ibid.*

## Receivership and Reorganization

although involving the refunding of certain equipment obligations did not imply even a temporary sacrifice. There were two classes of equipment obligations outstanding; those issued under the Philadelphia plan were paid in money, whereas the equipment mortgage bonds were refunded. For each $1,000 in equipment mortgage 5% bonds, the bondholder received $1,000 in new consolidated mortgage 4% bonds and $480 in new preferred stock. He was compelled to undergo a sacrifice of 1% in yearly income, but this was fully compensated for by the preferred stock bonus. Subsequently, with the success of the rejuvenated Norfolk and Western road, he had an increase in both income and principal.

Review of other reorganizations of the period [4] shows a general pattern of providing funds to pay off the earlier installments of equipment obligations, and of having the reorganized company assume the obligation of paying the later installments. There were a few delays; Baltimore and Ohio, for instance, extended for three years the final installment of one of its car trusts, increasing the interest rate from $4\frac{1}{2}$ percent to 5 percent.

In the first three decades of the present century there were numerous reorganizations which involved no sacrifice or delay for holders of equipment obligations, such as:

| | |
|---|---|
| Central Vermont | 1930 |
| Chicago, Milwaukee and St. Paul | 1927 |
| Chicago, Rock Island and Pacific | 1917 |
| Denver and Rio Grande Western | 1924 |
| Missouri, Kansas and Texas | 1923 |
| Missouri Pacific | 1917 |
| St. Louis and San Francisco | 1916 |

[4] E.g., Atchison, Topeka and Santa Fe; Baltimore and Ohio; Erie; Northern Pacific; and Union Pacific. Data from *Poor's Manual of*

At the same time there were instances of default, mostly temporary.

The Detroit, Toledo and Ironton Railway affords the first case. Formed in 1905 by reorganization of the Detroit Southern, the company defaulted on its bonds and went into receivership in 1908. The receiver met other series of equipment obligations, but defaulted on the Equipment Trust 4½ percent Notes and surrendered the pledged equipment to the trustee of that issue, thinking the road's equity in it too small to be worth preserving, especially as the road had enough rolling stock without it. The notes were not included in the eventual reorganization, but the holders were able to sell the equipment, in small lots, for enough to cover the debt.[5]

The Buffalo and Susquehanna Railway defaulted on its first mortgage bonds and went into receivership in 1910. Dewing [6] summarizes the matter in the following terms:

This was a very unfortunate venture which, reorganized as the Wellsville and Buffalo Railroad, proved such a failure that it was closed November, 1916, and dismantled. The old Buffalo and Susquehanna Railway had four issues of equipment obligations, A, B, C, D. Three were assumed by an allied company, the Buffalo and Susquehanna Railroad Corporation, which paid them all. The fourth equipment trust was not assumed. After considerable negotiation the equipment covered by it was sold to a syndicate of Buffalo men. This syndicate subsequently sold the equipment, and in order

---

*Railroads* (New York, Poor's Railroad Manual Company, annually from 1869).

[5] Kenneth Duncan, *Equipment Obligations* (New York, Appleton, 1924), p. 233.

[6] Dewing, *Corporation Securities,* p. 374, footnote bbb.

*Receivership and Reorganization* 73

to give a free title, deposited with the trustee a sum equivalent to the unpaid certificates and their interest to maturity.

The Wabash, whose operations extend from Buffalo to Kansas City, went into receivership in 1911. It had outstanding four series of equipment obligations, of which the receiver permitted the 4½ percent Notes Series C to default in 1912. In 1915, however, the holders were offered the choice of payment in cash, or new notes plus a small cash bonus. The other series were either provided for in the reorganization, or assumed by the new company and paid at maturity.[7]

The Wheeling and Lake Erie defaulted on some of its bonds and went into receivership in 1908. It had outstanding Twenty-Year 5 percent Equipment Bonds issued in 1902, on which a sinking fund was provided, to be used for the retirement of bonds or the purchase of additional equipment.[8] The receiver maintained interest and sinking fund payments for several years, eventually defaulting on the January 1, 1915, installment of sinking fund and July 1, 1915, interest.

After the certificates had been in default for over a year, the reorganization managers, in contemplation of the forthcoming reorganization, agreed to pay the back interest and to pay 35% of the face of the outstanding certificates in cash and to give new 4% Secured Sinking Fund Equipment Notes for the remaining 65%. These new notes were secured by the old unmatured equipment bonds, which in their turn were secured by the equity in the equipment. The reorganized company agreed to buy and cancel one-sixth of the new notes each year

[7] Duncan, *Equipment Obligations,* p. 237.   [8] *Ibid.,* p. 238.

until the entire issue was redeemed. . . . In the years following the receivership, the management of the reorganized road paid the refunded certificates in full.[9]

The Pere Marquette Railroad, whose properties were mostly in the state of Michigan, went into receivership in 1912. Payments on equipment obligations were maintained until early in March, 1914, when the court ordered discontinuance of principal and interest payments on funded obligations of every sort, and at about the same time the holders of outstanding equipment obligations discovered that the installments matured and paid during the receivership had not been canceled but were deposited as security for the receivers' certificates which had been issued to provide the funds for payment. Their protective committee undertook to establish the priority of the remaining installments, and obtained an order directing the receivers to issue receivers' certificates for them. When the reorganization was finally effected in 1917, all outstanding equipment obligations were paid off.[10]

The Chicago, Peoria and St. Louis Railroad went into receivership in 1914, defaulting on its junior bonds at that time and on its Prior (first) Lien Bonds in 1918. Payment of principal and interest on equipment trust notes was maintained until November 1, 1918; the installment of principal then due was paid in July, 1919, with interest; 1919 installments of interest and principal were paid May 1, 1920; and subsequent payments were made when due.[11]

[9] Dewing, *Corporation Securities*, p. 365, footnote mm.
[10] Duncan, *Equipment Obligations*, pp. 235, 236.
[11] *Ibid.*, pp. 232, 233; *Moody's Manual of Investments: Transportation*, 1922 (New York, Moody's Investors Service), p. 37; Paul Smith,

## Receivership and Reorganization 75

The Atlanta, Birmingham and Atlantic, a southeastern road of light traffic and little earning power, had the unhappy distinction of successive receiverships in 1909, 1915, and 1921. The 1914 reorganization, which ended the first of these, left equipment obligations undisturbed. The 1915 reorganization was so drastic that even the receivers' certificates were exchanged for income bonds, but the equipment obligations were paid off at par. For the third receivership the equipment debt, all held by the Director General of Railroads, was subject to various defaults and delays, but was finally paid in full in 1926 when the property was leased to Atlantic Coast Line.[12]

Chicago and Eastern Illinois went into receivership in 1915, defaulting interest on practically all its bonds within a year or two thereafter. Installments of equipment obligations due on and after February 1, 1915, were extended for three years, the interest rate being increased to 5½ percent (from 4½ percent and 5 percent) and a lien on the mortgaged lines (subject to certain underlying liens) added as additional security. The extended installments were paid as they matured, those which had not become due by the time of reorganization being assumed by the new company.[13]

The next testing period for equipment obligations, as for other securities, was the great depression of the

---

Jr., The Development of the Legal Status of American Railroad Equipment Securities (unpublished J.S.D. dissertation submitted at New York University, School of Law, March, 1930), p. 42.

[12] Duncan, *Equipment Obligations,* pp. 229–31; Smith, Development of Legal Status, pp. 41–42.

[13] *Moody's,* 1918, p. 210; *ibid.,* 1923, p. 143.

1930s, when so large a proportion of the country's railroad mileage was forced into receivership or reorganization. During and since that decade we have seen the following reorganizations, in some cases "voluntary," without default on principal or interest of equipment obligations: [14]

| | |
|---|---|
| Alton | 1947 |
| Ann Arbor | 1943 |
| Baltimore and Ohio | 1944 |
| Bangor and Aroostook | 1950 |
| Central of Georgia | 1948 |
| Chicago and Alton | 1931 |
| Central Railroad of New Jersey | 1949 |
| Chicago and Eastern Illinois | 1941 |
| Chicago Great Western | 1941 |
| Chicago, Indianapolis and Louisville | 1946 |
| Chicago and North Western | 1945 |
| Denver and Rio Grande Western | 1947 |
| Erie | 1941 |
| International Great Northern | 1956 |
| Lehigh Valley | 1949 |
| Long Island | 1954 |
| Minneapolis and St. Louis | 1943 |
| New Orleans, Texas and Mexico | 1956 |
| New York, New Haven and Hartford | 1947 |
| Western Pacific | 1946 |
| Wisconsin Central | 1954 |

Among those which did not maintain the scheduled payments was the Seaboard Air Line Railway, organized in 1900 as a consolidation of small lines in the southeastern states. In a previous reorganization, equipment obliga-

[14] Compilation by the writer from data in *Moody's*.

## Receivership and Reorganization

tions had been fully protected, being paid from funds raised by sale of receivers' certificates in 1908.[15] In the second proceeding, which began at the end of 1930, holders of maturing equipment obligations were offered a like amount of receivers' certificates, secured by pledge of the original obligations, maturing in 1945, with interest at 2 percent for the first three years, 3 percent for the next two, and 3½ percent thereafter. The receivers subsequently invited tenders of the certificates, thus retiring the greater part at an average price of 78, and eventually called the balance for payment at par.[16]

Wabash was another of the early casualties, defaulting on its junior bonds and going into receivership late in 1931. The receivers negotiated agreements with practically all the holders of equipment trust certificates by which maturing installments of principal were extended three years, interest payments being maintained; in 1938 all principal payments, including those previously deferred, were suspended, without interruption of interest, but in 1939 the entire balance of outstanding certificates was paid at par with funds provided by a loan from the Reconstruction Finance Corporation.[17]

Norfolk Southern, a small line extending from Hampton Roads into North Carolina, went into receivership in July, 1932, and defaulted the interest on all its bonds. Interest payments were maintained on its four small issues of equipment obligations, but principal installments were

[15] Dewing, *Corporation Securities,* p. 373, footnote aaa.

[16] John Stevenson, "Financing of Railroad Equipment," *The Analysts Journal,* IX (No. 5, November, 1953), 29.

[17] *Moody's,* 1938, pp. 1864–65; *ibid.,* 1939, pp. 1044–45.

not paid until 1935; thereafter payments were made promptly.[18]

St. Louis–San Francisco, whose lines extended from St. Louis and Kansas City southwest into Texas and southeast to Birmingham, Alabama, had a somewhat similar history. Going into receivership in November, 1932, it promptly defaulted on practically all its debt, including principal and interest of equipment obligations. In January, 1934, the court authorized purchase of matured notes and coupons on the equipment obligations at par as funds should become available; such purchases were started at the end of the month and proceeded with varying delays, payments being brought up to date in 1938 and made promptly thereafter.[19]

Missouri Pacific, another southwestern road, started reorganization proceedings at the end of March, 1933, defaulting on substantially all its bonds. Payments on equipment obligations were maintained, except for the May 1, 1933, and May 1, 1934 installments of principal on Series F, which were not paid until January, 1934, and June, 1934, respectively.[20]

Mobile and Ohio, which had gone into receivership in the middle of 1932, announced in January, 1935, a plan for postponement of principal installments on equipment debt maturing between October 31, 1934, and September 1, 1936. Agreements were signed and the plan declared operative by October 1, 1935, but all extended maturities

[18] *Moody's*, 1935, p. 595; *ibid.*, 1936, p. 1842.
[19] *Moody's*, 1939, p. 1718.  [20] *Moody's*, 1937, p. 1861.

*Receivership and Reorganization* 79

were retired by the end of October, 1936, and subsequent payments were made promptly.[21]

The Rock Island [22] in 1937 offered holders of equipment obligations an exchange into a like amount of trustees' certificates due 1947, carrying $3\frac{1}{2}$ percent interest and secured by pledge of the obligations exchanged, with a sinking fund calculated to retire the entire issue by maturity. In 1940 these certificates were called for payment at par, from the proceeds of a new issue.[23]

Chicago, Milwaukee, St. Paul and Pacific began reorganization proceedings in the summer of 1935, defaulting on substantially all its bonds. Interest payments on the equipment obligations were maintained, but maturing installments of principal were paid 20 percent when due, and a like amount at the end of each of the next four years; in 1940, the bankruptcy trustee paid the balance with funds raised by selling trustees' certificates.[24]

Florida East Coast Railway, suffering from a collapsing boom and increasing competition, rail [25] and highway, had gone into receivership in 1931. The equipment covered by the Series D Trust was deemed unnecessary for continued operation, and while the other equipment trusts were eventually paid in full, the receivers disaffirmed this trust in 1936. Repossession and sale of the equipment

[21] *Moody's,* 1940, p. 1292. [22] See above, Chapter IV.
[23] Stevenson, "Financing of Railroad Equipment," p. 28.
[24] *Ibid.*
[25] Seaboard Air Line Railway mileage in Florida had been greatly increased during the boom, including a line into Palm Beach and Miami.

netted only $440.58 per $1,000 certificate. The trustee proceeded to obtain a judgment against the railroad for the deficiency, but as an unsecured general claim necessarily junior to the mortgages on the road this appeared to have little value. However, the trustee also recovered a substantial judgment against the receivers for their use of the equipment and failure to repair, before disaffirmance; this permitted an additional distribution of $152.96 per certificate. Finally, in 1950, a settlement was reached for a partial payment on the deficiency claim, permitting a further distribution of $108.27 which increased the total to $701.81, or about 70 percent, net after expenses.[26]

The New York, Ontario, and Western case reviewed above [27] offers the only other recent instance in which an equipment lease was disaffirmed and the equipment repossessed. The 1945 trust, secured by nine 2,700 horsepower diesels, realized $282,737.68, net after expenses of sale, including fees of the equipment trustee and his counsel, against $453,000 unpaid principal, or approximately 62.4 percent, without allowing for several months' unpaid interest. The 1947 trust, secured by twenty diesels of 1,000 horsepower and seven of 1,500 horsepower, realized $1,557,876.26, or enough to cover all claims in full, including interest at the coupon rate to date of settlement, and to provide a small surplus to be turned over to the receiver.[28]

[26] *Moody's,* 1937, p. 153; 1950, p. 709; 1953, p. 123.
[27] See Chapter IV.
[28] U.S. District Court (Southern District of New York) Civil Number 116-204, United States of America, Plaintiff vs. Lewis D. Free-

Thus, within the present century there appear to have been only four cases in which holders of equipment obligations have had to repossess and sell the pledged equipment. In the Detroit, Toledo and Ironton and the Buffalo and Susquehanna cases discussed earlier in this chapter, the sale realized enough to protect the holders, as it did also in the case of the larger of the New York, Ontario and Western issues. The only serious losses were on the Florida East Coast Series D and the smaller Ontario trust, where the realizations worked out around 70 percent and 62 percent respectively, in each case without including accrued interest.

Of the various compromises or adjustments, the characteristic feature in recent decades has been delay in payment of part or all of the principal. Only in two cases (Seaboard and Rock Island) have equipment creditors been required to take a reduction of interest, and in none has their principal been scaled down. We have to go back into the last century, to the Norfolk and Western and the Denver and Rio Grande cases reviewed at the beginning of this chapter, to find instances of equipment holders having to take long-term bonds and preferred stock.

Of course, deferment of principal may mean a very real sacrifice. Obligations of comparatively short maturity are frequently, if not ordinarily, held in anticipation of specific need for cash at or about the due date. To such a holder, inability to liquidate (i.e., turn the holding into cash) at or about face value at the stipulated time may

---

man, Trustee *et al.:* final order dated July 9, 1957, directing acceptance of bids and distribution of proceeds.

mean a serious loss, even though the obligations are eventually paid in full. So we cannot ignore such cases, or consider eventual payment in full as an entirely satisfactory solution. To know that practically all equipment issues are eventually paid in full (the Florida East Coast Series D and the Ontario 1945 trust being two exceptions among hundreds, if not thousands, of cases) is interesting to the student and an important second line of defense to the investor, but the primary consideration of the latter may be his prospect of being paid in full, on time.

Such an investor is in a sense less interested in the specific arrangements to bail him out, generally without loss of either principal or interest, than in the hundreds of cases where there has not been even a temporary default. It is because equipment obligations offer the probability rather than the certainty of such punctual payment that they cannot be considered "riskless" investments, in the sense in which the word can be applied to United States government obligations of similar maturity. Nor does the record support the idea that the value of equipment obligations is independent of the credit of the issuing road. That credit is the investor's best assurance of punctuality, as distinguished from ultimate safety. In the event of financial embarassment, payment on even the best-secured issue may be delayed while the bankruptcy trustee is endeavoring to work out some compromise, and the equipment creditors are making up their minds whether to accept such a compromise or insist on full payment at the risk of having to repossess the equipment.[29]

[29] See above, pp. 56–58.

*CHAPTER VI*

# Equipment Trust Agreements

SINCE, as previously mentioned, practically all equipment trust certificates are now issued under the Philadelphia Plan, only agreements of that type will be discussed here.

The fundamental idea, as explained above, in Chapter III, is that the certificate holders—i.e., the investors who provide the funds—are protected by vesting in a trustee for their benefit the title to the equipment and the obligations of the railroad as lessee of the equipment. This was ordinarily accomplished by two separate, though related, agreements. There was first a lease to the railroad, from the trustee as owner or prospective owner of the equipment, and second a three-cornered trust agreement among the trustee, the railroad, and the "vendors" who were supplying the equipment. These vendors might be either the actual manufacturers, or nominees of the bankers or the railroad—particularly if some or all of the equipment was being built in railroad shops.

The lease covered the right of the railroad company to use the equipment, and its obligation to pay the stipulated rental, namely the amount of the down payment (generally 20 percent) on delivery, and further sums as and when required thereafter sufficient to cover expenses of the trust (and any taxes), scheduled installments of the certificates, and dividends thereon at the stipulated rate—the return being described as dividends rather than interest, to emphasize the idea that the certificates represent interests in the trust property and the rentals therefrom, rather than a loan of money. It stipulated that when, and only when, the rentals had provided funds for retirement of all the certificates, with dividends, and for defraying the other charges, the lease would terminate and the leased equipment be transferred to and become the property of the railroad or its nominee. It likewise contained the railroad's covenant to maintain and repair the equipment, to replace (at its own expense for account of the trustee) any units lost or destroyed, to have each unit permanently and conspicuously marked to show the trustee's ownership, to furnish the trustee annually (or oftener if requested) an accurate list and description of the equipment and repairs made or to be made, to permit inspection by the trustee or its agents, and not to assign or transfer the lease without consent of the trustee. Finally, it set forth the trustee's remedies in the event of default; its right to repossess and sell all or any part of the leased equipment, and the railroad's obligation to assemble and deliver the same.

The trust agreement was a three-party document covering the transfer of title from the vendors to the trustee, the issue of trust certificates to the vendors or upon their order for not more than a stipulated part (usually 80 percent) of the cost of the equipment, a description and specimens of the trust certificates and dividend warrants,

## Equipment Trust Agreements 85

the undertaking of the railroad to endorse on each certificate its guaranty of principal and dividends and to enter into the lease (actually the execution of the lease is generally simultaneous with that of the trust agreement), the remedies in event of default in somewhat more detail than in the lease, any provision for prepayment of certificates at the option of the railroad, and sundry provisions as to the rights and liabilities of the several parties.[1]

Although the arrangement just described is still extensively used, I have described it in the past tense because leading New York attorneys [2] have recently developed a

[1] Kenneth Duncan, *Equipment Obligations* (New York, Appleton, 1924), pp. 294-317, reprints in full the lease and the trust agreement, both dated August 1, 1913, covering the Illinois Central Equipment Trust Series B. Charles W. Gerstenberg, *Materials of Corporation Finance,* 3rd rev. ed. (New York, Prentice-Hall, 1915), pp. 313–19, reprints the trust agreement dated July 1, 1907, covering the Erie Railroad Car Trust Series "L." Robert L. Masson and Samuel S. Stratton, *Financial Instruments and Institutions: A Case Book* (New York, McGraw-Hill, 1938), pp. 75–81, reprints a somewhat condensed version of the trust agreement and lease covering the New York, New Haven and Hartford Equipment Trust of 1931.

Such leases and agreements, being matters of public record, can be inspected where they are on file, generally at state capitals (office of the secretary of state) in cases prior to 1952, and at Washington, D.C. (office of the Interstate Commerce Commission) since that time. The trustee, the railroad, the bankers who underwrote the sale of the issue, and their respective attorneys each have one or more copies of the agreements, and some of them may have a copy to spare. Copies of typical leases and trust agreements should be available in any extensive financial library (e.g., at universities which maintain schools of business, or at the larger metropolitan banks).

[2] Leonard D. Adkins of Cravath, Swaine & Moore, in association with Thomas O'G. FitzGibbon of Davis Polk Wardwell Sunderland & Kiendl, and others.

simplified form, combining the lease and trust agreement in a single document, and eliminating vendors.[3]

The new form, which is one agreement between railroad and trustee, begins by reciting that the former has contracted or will contract for construction and transfer to the trustee of the equipment involved, that a specified principal amount of equipment trust certificates is to be issued and sold to provide a fund applicable by the trustee to part payment for the trust equipment (the balance of the cost to be paid by the railroad as advance rental), that certificates, dividend warrants, and the endorsed guaranty of the railroad are to follow substantially the texts set forth (Appendixes A, B, and C), and that the railroad and the trustee enter the agreement to secure payment of the certificates and dividends and to evidence the rights of certificate holders.

Article I sets forth a series of definitions, of which only two call for comment. The definition of equipment, necessary to cover such cases as replacement of units lost or destroyed, has long specified new standard gauge railroad equipment other than work equipment (i.e., cranes, main-

[3] Mr. FitzGibbon, in a letter to me dated August 10, 1956, wrote, "Adkins and I, as lawyers, might like to go the whole way and change the lease provisions into those of a conditional sale," to which I replied, ". . . the Philadelphia Plan has such prestige, is so easy to explain (at least superficially) to the uninformed, and is so widely understood (or thought to be understood) by people who may have difficulty in grasping the subtleties of retaining title under conditional sale, that I think you are bound to run into substantial opposition from prospective purchasers—particularly purchasers with a view to resale, such as investment bankers." They evidently got similar answers from other sources, including the all-important underwriters.

## Equipment Trust Agreements

tenance cars, etc.); now it is becoming customary also to exclude passenger cars, and in some cases flat cars used for carrying highway trailers or trailer bodies—commonly called "piggyback" equipment. The fair value of any unit, likewise necessary as a basis of replacement, is defined as cost less depreciation at a stipulated rate, thereby eliminating any necessity of appraisal or reference to an outside (possibly changing) authority, such as rules of the Interstate Commerce Commission or the Master Car Builders.

Article II spells out in detail the provisions for the issue of certificates in accordance with their terms and with the preceding recitals, and for the replacement, upon satisfactory evidence and indemnity, of certificates lost, stolen, mutilated, or destroyed.

Article III covers the acquisition of the equipment by the trustee, the railroad assigning its interest in the construction contracts to the trustee and undertaking to accept delivery as agent of the trustee, and the trustee making payment against such delivery (from the fund evidenced by the certificates plus the advance rental paid by the railroad) on receipt of documents satisfactorily evidencing delivery, cost, title, and marking.

Article IV covers lease of all the equipment to the railroad for the term of years covered by the longest series of certificates, and the road's agreement to pay as rental the 20 percent down payment, plus sums sufficient to cover the expenses of the trust (including any taxes) and the dividend warrants and principal installments; also to mark the equipment conspicuously and permanently in evidence of the trustee's ownership, to maintain it in good order and repair, to replace (or deposit with the trustee cash to the value of) any equipment worn out, lost, or destroyed, and to furnish the trustee when requested, and at least once in each calendar year, a list and description of the trust equipment in service, undergoing (or awaiting) repairs, lost, destroyed, or replaced during the year, with evidence of its proper marking. The railroad further agrees not to assign its rights under the lease, or sublet any part of the trust equipment, without the consent of the trustee; the trustee agrees that the railroad, so long as it is not in default, may use the trust equipment (and permit its use on connecting and other lines in the usual interchange of traffic) and that when, and only when, all payments under the lease are completed such payments shall be applied as purchase money in full payment for the equipment, title to which shall thereupon vest in the railroad, the trustee giving such evidence of title as may reasonably be requested. The trustee likewise agrees to give releases covering any equipment which shall have become worn out or unsuitable, upon request of the railroad and deposit of its value in cash (or substitution of new equipment), and the railroad agrees to indemnify the trustee against any and all claims, particularly those arising out of the use of any patented invention, and to comply with all lawful acts, rules, and orders of the Interstate Commerce Commission or other governmental authorities.

Article V covers the remedies in event of default. The trustee may, and upon request of holders of a stipulated

## Equipment Trust Agreements

percentage of the certificates shall, declare the entire amount of the rental (excepting *future* dividends but including future installments of principal) due and payable; it may repossess all or any part of the trust equipment, which the railroad undertakes to assemble, deliver, and store for the trustee without charge, and may lease or sell the same. No such repossession, lease, sale or withdrawal, or any other act or omission of the trustee or the security holders, is to affect the obligation of the railroad under its lease or the endorsed guaranty; presentation and demand under the guaranty are expressly waived, and it is stipulated that the various remedies shall be cumulative rather than exclusive.

Article VI covers additional covenants and agreements of the company—to pay the expenses and compensation of the trustee and the rentals and other amounts provided in the agreement; to pay principal and dividends of each certificate; to pay any tax or similar charge that might become a lien upon the trust equipment; to pay all incidental expenses in connection with the preparation and execution of the trust certificates and dividend warrants and the preparation, execution, recording, and filing of the agreement and any documents necessary in connection therewith; and to file the agreement with the Interstate Commerce Commission in accordance with Section 20c of the Interstate Commerce Act.[4]

Article VII concerns the trustee—its acceptance of the trusts imposed by the agreement, and its covenants to perform the same, to apply the rentals received for the

[4] See above, pp. 46–48.

purposes specified, to maintain registration and transfer books; its freedom from various liabilities and its right, in its discretion, to take no action unless requested and indemnified by holders of a stipulated percentage of the certificates; its right to hold the trust funds on deposit without interest, or at such interest as it and the railroad may agree upon, and its duty to invest the funds in United States government securities at the direction of the railroad; its right to employ agents and attorneys and to receive from the railroad compensation for its services and reimbursement for its expenses; and its right to resign the trust and turn it over to a qualified successor, as defined.

Article VIII contains miscellaneous provisions, such as the ways in which notice or demands are to be served on the respective parties, and in which ownership of certificates is to be established if and when necessary, and stipulations that each of the several counterparts of the agreement is to be considered an original, and that all of them together constitute but one document, and that the agreement and the rights of all parties thereunder are to be governed by the laws of the State of New York.[5]

[5] Among the agreements executed in this new form in 1957 were:
Alabama Great Southern, Series K.
Ann Arbor Railroad, Series C.
Cincinnati, New Orleans and Texas Pacific, Series L.
Gulf, Mobile and Ohio, Series H.
Southern Railway, Series UU.
Wabash Railroad, Series I.

All these agreements are on file with the Interstate Commerce Commission in Washington, D.C., and can be inspected there; presumably they can also be inspected at the office of the trustee, the railroad, the underwriters, or their respective attorneys, some of whom may have a copy to spare.

## Equipment Trust Agreements

This last point may be important in various connections, one of the most obvious being the negotiability of the certificates. Equipment trust certificates do not comply with the technical provisions of the Negotiable Instrument Law, being obligations payable only from a specified fund rather than unconditional promises to pay,[6] but under the laws of New York negotiability may be conferred by agreement.[7]

No mention has been made of call provisions—i.e., provision for prepayment of the certificates at stipulated prices at the option of the railroad. Such options were not common even a generation ago; the so-called Government Equipment Trusts of January 15, 1920 [8] gave the respective borrowers the option of calling their obligations for prepayment at 103, and twelve of the issues were so retired between 1923 and 1929, but of the other equipment issues outstanding in 1928 very few of the railroad ones were callable, call provisions being found mostly in so-called marine equipment trusts and private car line issues.[9]

In recent years, such prepayment or call provisions have been practically unknown in equipment trust cer-

[6] The unconditional nature of the railroad's guaranty does not alter the character of the certificate. Fidelity & Deposit Co. of Md. v. Andrews, 244 Mich. 159, 221 N.W. 114 (1928), as cited by Paul Smith, Jr., The Development of the Legal Status of American Railroad Equipment Securities (unpublished J.S.D. dissertation submitted at New York University, School of Law, March, 1950), p. 78.

[7] New York Personal Property Law, Sections 260–262, as cited *ibid.*

[8] See above, Chapter III.

[9] These observations of the writer are based on a review of the issues listed in *Equipment Trust Securities (Eighth Series)*, Evans, Stillman and Co., New York, 1928.

tificates. Of 190 issues in the calendar years 1953–56, only nine carried call provisions; in each of these (obligations of the Seaboard, the Virginian, and the Wabash) the last five maturities were subject to redemption without premium, in inverse order of maturity, after the first five years. Of the 63 issues in the first nine months of 1957, which included financing by all three of these roads, none carried call provisions.

This is the more surprising because call provisions are almost universal in other corporate securities, and regulatory commissions sometimes insist upon them as a matter of policy.[10] The divergence in practice appears primarily to reflect two factors. In the first place, during a large part of the period since the First World War the railroads have been glad to get credit on any reasonable terms, and the Interstate Commerce Commission has necessarily been more concerned with keeping the lenders happy, so that the railroads could get credit, than with seeing that the borrowers reserved for themselves the option of refunding the debt if and when money should become available on more favorable terms. In the second place, we have the power of inertia: a custom well established is hard to change. After years in which equipment trust certificates have habitually been issued in noncallable form, investors come to expect that form, bankers hold it forth as one of the attractions of such investments, underwriters shy

[10] James C. Sargent, member of Securities and Exchange Commission, addressing Legal Committee Meeting of Edison Electric Institute, at Buck Hill Falls, Pennsylvania, June 20, 1957. See *The Commercial and Financial Chronicle* CLXXXVI, 5654 (July 11, 1957), esp. p. 26.

away from any proposal to insert call provisions in new issues (especially under competitive bidding, where the margin of profit hardly encourages innovations which may be hard to merchandise), and borrowers console themselves with the reflection that the serial maturities and short average life of the issues would minimize the profits on refunding in any event.[11]

We have spoken of the down payment as being usually 20 percent, so that the certificates represent 80 percent of the cost of the equipment, and of the maturities as being equal installments (annual or semiannual), usually over a fifteen-year period. These are well established practices, but by no means universal; they can be discussed together because they are logically related, rapid retirement tending to correct or offset any deficiency in the initial payment.

The present practice dates from about the time of the First World War. Before that, ten-year retirement schedules, with 10 percent down payments, were quite common. The change presumably reflects the greater durability of steel or steel-underframe equipment, which could be expected to have a useful life far beyond ten years, together with the higher cost of such equipment. This higher cost

[11] We have a similar reflection of the power of inertia, in the opposite direction, in the acquiescence of lenders in comparatively low call prices on corporate bonds and preferred stocks; they might grumble about the unfairness of provisions which give every advantage to the borrower, enabling him to take advantage of any substantial decline in interest rates, while the lender remains tied to his contract no matter how much rates may advance, but until the shortage of investment funds became really acute in 1957 they generally wound up by consenting to the established custom.

made the longer retirement schedule desirable, to reduce the drain on corporate funds, and at the same time made the larger down payment necessary, especially in view of the possibility that the war and postwar price levels might prove temporary and of the obvious fact that the longer term provided more opportunity for changes in the price level. The depression of the thirties provided a vivid demonstration of the possibility of price declines, and no doubt served to crystallize opinion against any return to lower down payments.

The Chesapeake and Ohio sold equipment trust certificates for practically the full value of the equipment in 1948,[12] but the credit of the road was such that it could have sold unsecured notes without difficulty. The Interstate Commerce Commission was reluctant to give its authorization, expressing concern lest such a practice should lower public confidence in equipment obligations and impair their usefulness as a vehicle for future financing.[13] The Chesapeake did not repeat the experiment, nor did other roads follow its example.

Few of the other issues since V-J Day have involved down payments substantially less than 20 percent.[14] A number have carried down payments of 25 percent [15] and

[12] *Moody's Manual of Investments: Transportation,* 1957, pp. 907, 908, items 10–13 inclusive.

[13] 267 I.C.C. 796 (1948), as cited by Smith, Development of Legal Status.

[14] None since 1952; Illinois Terminal in July and Bangor and Aroostook in September of that year.

[15] E.g., Southern Pacific, Series JJ in June, 1953, through VV in October, 1956; Seaboard through Series Q in May, 1957; Rock Island, Norfolk and Western in 1957; Reading Series V in 1956; Pennsylvania in 1955 and 1956.

## Equipment Trust Agreements

a few 33 percent.[16] The larger down payments undoubtedly encouraged purchasers where there was any shadow, deserved or not, on the carrier's credit (e.g., roads in reorganization at the time, such as St. Louis, Brownsville and Mexico, or recently, such as the New Haven) or on the value of the equipment, as in the case of passenger cars, but there is no evidence that it had any material effect on the marketability of such issues as Southern Pacific. Consequently the 20 percent routine seems to be firmly established and increasingly popular; more than 80 percent of the issues in the first nine months of 1957 were on the basis of 20 percent down payments (including several roads which had used larger payments in previous years) as compared with about 66 percent in 1954–55 and less than 60 percent in 1953.[17]

Almost none of the issues during the same period have carried maturities beyond fifteen years. Among the obvious reasons for this are the chilling experience of the longer Wheeling and Lake Erie equipments;[18] the limitations in a few of the state statutes governing institutional investments;[19] and particularly such sharp reminders of the dangers of obsolescence as the almost complete displacement of the steam locomotive, after a century of supremacy, by diesel-electric power within little more than a decade.

There have been, and continue to be, a number of issues

[16] E.g., Southern Pacific Series HH in 1952 and Series II in 1953; Gulf, Mobile and Ohio in 1952.
[17] Compilation by the writer from data furnished by Salomon Bros. & Hutzler, New York, N.Y.
[18] See above, Chapter V.
[19] E.g., New York Banking Law, Section 235, subdivision 7(c).

on which the retirement schedule runs to a shorter period of years, such as ten [20] or twelve.[21] As in the case of larger down payments, the effect (if any) of such schedules on the marketability of the issues does not seem conspicuous enough to encourage their widespread use. While increased down payments and shorter maturities reduce the total of interest payments in direct proportion, most railroads have more pressing needs for their cash than the reduction of equipment debt, which is probably the cheapest of all their borrowing, and do not think it advisable to increase the burden of down payment and/or annual installments unless the result is a lower rate of interest, rather than just the lower total resulting from the reduced amount and/or term of the borrowing.

Actually, shortening the maturity appears to be the most effective way of increasing the intrinsic strength of equipment obligations. Table 4 shows the ratio of certificates outstanding at the start of each year to the original cost of the equipment, on various assumptions as to down payment and maturity schedules. Comparison of columns 2 and 3 shows that increasing the down payment from 20 percent to 25 percent simply reduces the amount of certificates outstanding at each date by one sixteenth, not a very formidable differential. Turning to column 5, we find that reducing the equal annual installments from fifteen to twelve reduces the outstanding balance of certificates by margins which rise from one sixteenth (64–60)

[20] Southern Railway, Alabama Great Southern Railway, and Cincinnati, New Orleans and Texas Pacific Railway in 1957.
[21] Chicago, Rock Island and Pacific Series P in 1955 and Series Q in 1956.

at the start of the fourth year to one sixth (48–40) at the start of the seventh year and to much larger amounts thereafter—differentials which should represent a really substantial increase in the safety of the investment. Comparing columns 5 and 3, it will be seen that any time after the fourth year the twelve-year series with the conventional 20 percent down payment is also in a stronger position than a fifteen-year series with a 25 percent down payment.

Down payments of $33\frac{1}{3}$ percent reduce the balance of certificates outstanding at each date by one sixth (column 4 minus column 2), a really formidable margin, which column 5 would not match until the start of the seventh year. It would appear then, that down payments in such an amount really do give the investor increased protection, especially if there should be any danger of trouble in the earlier years, but that increasing the down payment to 25 percent is less effective than shortening the maturity by a few years.

Along the same lines, column 6 shows that the old-fashioned schedule of ten-year retirement with only 10 percent down payment actually gives the investor better protection from the start of the fourth year than does the 20 percent fifteen-year schedule now customary. We may conclude that the latter represents primarily the convenience of the borrower; if the lender has any doubt about the credit, his protection would be best effected by an accelerated maturity schedule if the outlook is clear for a few years ahead, or a one-third down payment if the borrower might be in trouble at an early date.

TABLE 4. RATIO OF CERTIFICATES OUTSTANDING AT START OF EACH YEAR TO ORIGINAL COST OF EQUIPMENT, ON VARIOUS ASSUMPTIONS AS TO DOWN PAYMENT AND MATURITY SCHEDULE

*(All Figures for Down Payments and Certificates Outstanding in Percent)*

| 1 | 2 | 3 | 4 | 5 | 6 | 7 |
|---|---|---|---|---|---|---|
| Down payment | 20 | 25 | 33⅓ | 20 | 10 | None |
| Number of equal annual installments | 15 | 15 | 15 | 12 | 10 | 10 |
| 1st year | 80.00 | 75.00 | 66.67 | 80.00 | 90.00 | 100.00 |
| 2nd year | 74.67 | 70.00 | 62.23 | 73.33 | 81.00 | 90.00 |
| 3rd year | 69.33 | 65.00 | 57.79 | 66.67 | 72.00 | 80.00 |
| 4th year | 64.00 | 60.00 | 53.34 | 60.00 | 63.00 | 70.00 |
| 5th year | 58.67 | 55.00 | 48.90 | 53.33 | 54.00 | 60.00 |
| 6th year | 53.33 | 50.00 | 44.44 | 46.67 | 45.00 | 50.00 |
| 7th year | 48.00 | 45.00 | 40.00 | 40.00 | 36.00 | 40.00 |
| 8th year | 42.67 | 40.00 | 35.55 | 33.33 | 27.00 | 30.00 |
| 9th year | 37.33 | 35.00 | 31.11 | 26.67 | 18.00 | 20.00 |
| 10th year | 32.00 | 30.00 | 26.67 | 20.00 | 9.00 | 10.00 |
| 11th year | 26.67 | 25.00 | 22.22 | 13.33 | .... | .... |
| 12th year | 21.33 | 20.00 | 17.77 | 6.67 | .... | .... |
| 13th year | 16.00 | 15.00 | 13.33 | .... | .... | .... |
| 14th year | 10.67 | 10.00 | 8.89 | .... | .... | .... |
| 15th year | 5.33 | 5.00 | 4.44 | .... | .... | .... |

Shorter maturity schedules may be promoted by current proposals for rebuilding that amounts practically to replacement of diesel-electric locomotives at a comparatively early date, around the twelfth year of their life. General Motors, having "dieselized" the railroads,[22] is now urging conversion or upgrading into practically new

[22] Most diesel-electric locomotives, and nearly all the older ones, are the product of General Motors Corporation, Electro-Motive Division. Data in this paragraph are taken from presentation by N. C. Dezendorf, Vice President, before The New York Society of Security Analysts, October 19, 1956, reprinted by General Motors, with exhibits, in a pamphlet entitled *Locomotive Upgrading*.

units as more productive than rebuilding in kind when the second cycle of major maintenance replacement begins. The first cycle, replacing such parts as engines, generators, traction motors, and auxiliaries about the sixth year of use, can be accomplished without taking the locomotive out of service long, but the second cycle, which also involves reworking trucks, structures, control apparatus, and running gear, involves shopping the complete locomotive. Electro-Motive, taking as an example its first main line freight locomotive, the 1,350 horsepower Model FT, urges that the economic overhaul of such a unit is its conversion into a 1,750 horsepower GP9, reusing in the new unit such long life engine, control, and motor parts, batteries, and truck assemblies, as can be satisfactorily remanufactured and modernized. The rebuilt unit carries Electro-Motive's new locomotive warranty, it has fully a third greater capacity, and its net cost (after crediting what the road would have had to spend on overhaul without conversion) is around $100,000, on which the savings (chiefly elimination of train-miles through greater hauling capacity) are estimated to be around 17 percent annually.

The first public financing based on such rebuilt locomotives was the offering of $1,335,000 Chicago and North Western Railway 5½ percent Equipment Trust Certificates in February, 1957. A copy of the offering circular is shown as Appendix D. It will be seen that the certificates represent 70 percent of the cost of twelve 1,750 horsepower locomotives model GP9, the railroad obtaining cash for the down payment by selling to the manufacturer a like number of ten-year-old F3 locomotives, "some of the components of which, when remanufactured, may be used in the locomotives to be delivered under this Trust." The price of the GP9 locomotives with remanufactured parts is stated to be 10 percent less than that of similar locomotives with entirely new components. In connection with General Motors' standard warranty on the locomotives, the railroad exhibits to prospective buyers of the certificates the builder's letter of February 5, 1957, which states:

We give this warranty because we regard the GP-9's to be delivered to you as equivalent, by all standards of equality in respect of materials and manufacture and in operating performance, to the same model locomotive as built by us under [new locomotive] Specification No. 8031.

The certificates were offered for competitive bidding and drew bids from the usual two syndicates.[23] The successful bidders, headed by Halsey, Stuart & Co., report no difficulty in disposing of the issue at the prices shown in Appendix C.[24]

However, before similar financing was arranged for twenty more locomotives in June, it was thought desirable to remove any doubt as to their status under statutes, such as the New York Banking Law,[25] which specify "new standard-gauge rolling stock." Counsel for the railroad company argued that "although certain parts in the Locomotives have been previously utilized, each locomotive it-

[23] See below, Chapter IX, second paragraph.
[24] Statement to the writer by George Polley, a partner of Dick & Merle-Smith, one of the underwriters.
[25] Section 235, subdivision 7(c).

self is new," citing various judicial decisions on what constitutes a new building, pointing out that for years freight cars containing reconditioned materials and parts have been considered "new standard-gauge rolling stock," quoting the Association of American Railroads definition of "new" cars, and explaining that (on the basis of information furnished by General Motors):

The process is the same as that for building a new locomotive and is in no sense a mere rebuilding or overhauling operation . . . all components of remanufactured locomotives are either completely new or are of the same quality as new equipment, and, with the exception of these utilized components, the remanufactured locomotives are built in accordance with the same specifications as completely new GP-9 units.[26]

The Banking Department replied:

This Department is willing to accept your opinion, embodied in your letter of June 13, 1957, that "remanufactured" locomotives described in such opinion and sold to the subject railroad with the manufacturer's standard warranty for new equipment, should be regarded as "new" for the purposes of Section 235, subd. 7(c) of the Banking Law.

The fact that such locomotives may contain certain reusable parts from other locomotives purchased by the manufacturer from the same railroad, or from another railroad, is not considered objectionable, if the above-mentioned standard warranty for new equipment is obtained.[27]

[26] Letter from Davis Polk Wardwell Sunderland & Kiendl to Department of Banking, State of New York, under date of June 13, 1957.
[27] Letter from John J. Moynahan, Assistant to Deputy Superintendent, Banking Department, to Thomas O'G. FitzGibbon of Davis Polk Wardwell Sunderland & Kiendl, under date of June 14, 1957.

Equipment trust certificates are rarely issued against equipment which cannot be qualified as "new," but there were such cases both before and after the Second World War. In February, 1949, the Chicago, Indianapolis and Louisville, better known as the Monon, sold $4,500,000 equipment trust certificates against new equipment costing $844,533 and used equipment stated to have a book value of $6,554,803 ($6,994,768 original cost less $439,966 depreciation). The used equipment, all held under conditional sale contracts to be paid from proceeds of the certificates, was described as freight cars and diesel-electric locomotives delivered subsequent to October 1, 1946, and passenger cars originally built as hospital cars for the United States Army in 1944 and converted into passenger cars in the railroad's own shops after January 6, 1947. The certificates, maturing in fifteen equal annual installments, represented about 61 percent of aggregate cost, less depreciation, or 46 percent of estimated replacement cost.[28]

In April, 1948, Illinois Central sold $14,000,000 equipment trust certificates issued against equipment not more than five years old, stated to have an original cost of $20,339,847, a book value (cost less depreciation to April 1, 1948) of $18,884,469, and a replacement value of approximately $25,600,000; the average age of the equipment, weighted on the basis of cost, was stated to be approximately two and one fourth years. The certificates represented not more than 75 percent of the depreciated value and matured in equal semiannual installments over

[28] Circular of Salomon Bros. & Hutzler *et al.*, dated February 11, 1949.

*Equipment Trust Agreements* 103

a period of ten years.[29] The financing was made possible by the fact that the railroad owned the equipment free and clear, without any mortgage or other lien.

Absence of a formidable "after-acquired property" clause in the Illinois Central mortgages was evidently an important factor in the issue of $15,000,000 4 percent Equipment Trust Certificates Series Q to the Federal Emergency Administration of Public Works in 1934, of which $13,900,000 were purchased from the Reconstruction Finance Corporation by investment bankers and reoffered in December, 1936. The proceeds of the certificates were stated to have been "used in large part, to rebuild, reconstruct, or recondition equipment and for the purchase of new equipment." By the terms of the Lease and Assignment, as amended, the railroad assigned to the trustee of Series Q its right to receive, upon expiration of existing equipment trusts, title to the equipment currently subject to other agreements; and at the time of reoffering the security was stated to include new equipment costing over $1,500,000 (including one locomotive still to be delivered), $527,000 cash in the hands of the trustee, and used equipment having a depreciated value exceeding $28,000,000, a total exceeding $30,000,000, or more than twice the original amount of the issue.[30]

[29] Circular of Halsey, Stuart & Co., Inc. *et al.,* dated Chicago, April 15, 1948, with attached tabulation.

[30] Circular of Salomon Bros. & Hutzler and Stroud & Company Incorporated, dated December 12, 1936.

*CHAPTER VII*

## Conditional Sale Contracts

CONDITIONAL sale contracts are in some respects less complicated, in others more complex, than equipment trust agreements.

They are less complicated in that no trustee is involved. The largest lender may act as agent for the others, or an independent agent may be appointed to hold title, receive and distribute payments, and deal generally with the builder and the railroad on behalf of the lenders, but this is strictly an agency, not a trusteeship. The number of lenders being limited, the agent can and does look to them for any necessary instructions, whereas the trustee of equipment trust certificates, which may have innumerable holders and are generally in bearer form, must exercise such discretion and initiative as may reasonably be expected in protecting the interest of the holders. A considerable part of the trust agreement is devoted to spelling out the duties and responsibilities of the trustee, and attempting to limit those responsibilities, and in spite of all the "exculpatory" clauses on which the trustee and its counsel may insist, the trusteeship involves, in the very nature of things, real and unavoidable responsibilities far beyond a mere agency.

Since the conditional sale contract is not intended to

## Conditional Sale Contracts

be negotiable, it omits the trust agreement's elaborate provisions governing the negotiability of certificates, replacement of those lost, stolen, or destroyed, and the maintenance of paying and transfer agencies. On the other hand, the contracts are more varied, and sometimes more complex, than trust agreements because they can be and are tailored to the particular case, containing provisions for deferred payment, price adjustment, or prepayment which would be inappropriate, perhaps unworkable, in an issue of equipment trust certificates.

Conditional sale contracts usually involve two or more separate but related agreements. The first of these is the actual sale contract, by which the railroad agrees to buy the specified equipment from the builder (or vendor) and to make payment for same as agreed. The second is the assignment of this contract to the lenders or their agent; if the lenders are not parties to this assignment, there will be a third agreement, between agent and lenders, by which the lenders agree to furnish the funds and the agent agrees to hold title to the contract for the benefit of the lenders in proportion to their respective investments.

The underlying conditional sale agreement begins by setting forth that the builder has contracted to construct (or the vendor to have constructed), sell, and deliver to the railroad, and the latter has agreed to purchase, the equipment described at the price and dates set forth. Sometimes it also sets forth at this point that builder [1]

---

[1] Throughout this discussion, the word "builder" includes the alternative "(or vendor)," and (unless otherwise indicated by the context) the successor "assignee."

and railroad have agreed that this agreement shall exclusively and completely state the rights of both parties, superseding all other agreements, oral or written, with respect to the equipment.

Then the agreement spells out the terms of payment in detail, beginning with the down payment (if any), the freight charges to point of delivery, and any excess of actual purchase price over the estimated price on which the financing is based. It is provided that if the agreement shall have been assigned (i.e., to the lenders or to their agent) the railroad's obligation for this excess shall be an unsecured debt, for which the builder is to have no lien on the equipment; in other words, nothing is to stand in the way of the assignee's claim on the equipment as security for the deferred installments.

The deferred installments, ordinarily in equal amounts at convenient intervals (e.g., semiannual) over a fifteen-year period, are ordinarily specified to carry interest at the stipulated rate from the "closing date" for each "group" of equipment, a group being defined in terms of a minimum number (or value) of cars or locomotives, to avoid the inconvenience of too frequent closings. The closing date is set by the railroad, on stipulated notice (e.g., five business days) to all parties, not more than a stipulated time (e.g., ten business days) after the builder's presentation of invoices and certificates of acceptance covering the equipment involved. In actual practice the builder gets payment in full on that date, having assigned the agreement, as explained below, for a sum equal to the principal amount of the deferred installments—

## Conditional Sale Contracts

the railroad having agreed, in negotiating the deal, on an interest rate acceptable to the lenders. Here and elsewhere in the agreements it is generally stipulated that any overdue payments shall carry interest, to the extent legally enforceable, at 6 percent from the due date.

The railroad agrees to pay promptly all taxes, assessments, and licenses involved, and to keep the equipment free and clear of all taxes and assessments which might result in a lien upon it, reserving, however, the right to contest same in good faith by appropriate legal proceedings as long as nonpayment does not adversely affect the property or rights of the builder. There is sometimes a similar clause to cover any other "sums claimed by any party . . . which if unpaid might become a lien or charge upon the Equipment . . . or any unit thereof, equal or superior to the title of the Manufacturer." [2]

The builder retains full legal title to and property in the equipment (and any additions thereto or replacements thereof), notwithstanding delivery to the railroad and use and possession by the latter, until the railroad has completed its payments and carried out its agreements. When, and only when, the purchase price has been paid in full, with interest, and all other obligations of the railroad under the agreement completed, title to the equipment shall pass to and vest in the railroad, and the builder if requested will execute and deliver an appropriate bill of sale and appropriate instruments to make clear upon

[2] Conditional Sale Agreement, dated as of October 1, 1956, by and between Pullman-Standard Car Manufacturing Company and The Kansas City Southern Railway Company, paragraph 14.

the public records the railroad's title to the equipment. The railroad, so long as it is not in default, is entitled to possession and use of the equipment on its own lines, or on connecting or other lines in through service and the ordinary interchange of traffic, but undertakes not to let any unit pass out of its control except to that extent, and not to lease the equipment or assign its rights under the agreement.

The railroad agrees not to mark the equipment in any fashion that would imply ownership by the railroad, but may cause it to be lettered with the name or initials of the railroad or otherwise appropriately marked for identification. It agrees not to change the identifying numbers of the equipment without consent of the builder and prior notice to him. It generally agrees to mark each unit of equipment, distinctly, permanently and conspicuously on each side, in letters not less than one inch in height, with the name of the builder, followed by the word "Owner," or other appropriate phrase designated by the builder; sometimes there is merely an agreement to so mark the equipment if and when requested by the builder, and to bear the expense of any charge or litigation resulting from the absence of such marking.[3]

The agreement may or may not provide for insurance. Such provision is obviously more important in an agreement covering a small number of expensive units, such as locomotives or passenger cars, than in one covering a greater number of less expensive units, such as freight

[3] Louisville and Nashville agreement, dated as of December 1, 1952, carrying 3¼ percent interest.

## Conditional Sale Contracts

cars; and more important with a weak borrower than with one which is clearly good for its obligation to promptly replace or pay for units lost, damaged, or destroyed. This latter obligation is universal, making suitable provision for the payment to be made if replacement is not in kind —the unpaid installments of purchase price on the unit involved, for instance, or its cost less depreciation at some stipulated rate, such as $\frac{1}{3}$ of one percent per month— and its application to purchase of new units or payment on the outstanding balance of debt. This payment may be used to reduce the final installment, or applied to pro rata reduction of all the installments, or (less desirably) to reduction of the earliest installment.

The railroad undertakes to maintain the equipment in good order and repair at its own expense, to comply with all lawful rules and orders of the Interstate Commerce Commission and any other legislative, executive, administrative or judicial body having jurisdiction, and to make at its own expense any alteration necessary to comply with such laws and rules, but reserves the right to contest in good faith, in any reasonable manner which does not adversely affect the property or rights of the builder, the validity and application of any such law or rule. It agrees to furnish the builder annually an accurate inventory and description of the equipment, a record of any units lost, destroyed, or irreparably damaged and of the units acquired in replacement, and such similar information as the builder may reasonably request. The builder has the right, but no obligation, to inspect the equipment and the railroad's record thereof each year.

The railroad agrees to indemnify the builder against all losses, damages, liabilities, and claims arising from retention of title to the equipment by the builder or use and operation thereof by the railroad, this covenant to remain in force notwithstanding full payment of the purchase price and conveyance of the equipment, or termination of the agreement in any manner whatever. The railroad bears the risk of, and is not released from its obligations in the event of, any damage to or destruction of any or all of the equipment. The builder is not relieved of its warranty on material and workmanship, but it is expressly provided that the rights of any assignee to the unpaid balance of the purchase price, with interest, and the other rights assigned shall not be subject to any defense, counterclaim, or offset arising from any claim of the railroad against the builder; all such obligations, however arising, are to be enforceable only against the builder himself.

The builder indemnifies the railroad against any and all claims and liabilities, including royalty payments and counsel fees, arising out of alleged patent infringements, except as to designs, articles, and materials specified by the railroads; as to these latter the railroad indemnifies the builder.

The railroad undertakes to have the agreement and the first assignment thereof (and any supplements to either) filed and recorded at its expense with the Interstate Commerce Commission in accordance with Section 20c of the Interstate Commerce Act,[4] and will see to any

[4] See above, pp. 46–48.

## Conditional Sale Contracts

other instruments and recording required by law or reasonably requested by the builder for further protection, and will furnish the builder evidence of such recording, with a satisfactory opinion of counsel.

The railroad undertakes to pay all reasonable costs, charges, and expenses, except counsel fees of the builder himself, but including fees and expenses of counsel for the first assignee and of anyone acquiring interests in the first assignment (i.e., the lenders and their agent).

It is specified that the agreement shall be construed in accordance with the laws of a designated state, generally New York; that it may be executed in any number of counterparts, each of which shall be deemed an original and all of which together shall constitute one and the same contract; that the railroad waives, to the extent permitted by law, statutory or legal requirements of every kind with respect to enforcement of the builder's rights, together with any right of redemption; and that any provision prohibited by any applicable law of any state, or which by any applicable law of any state would convert the agreement into anything other than an agreement of conditional sale, shall be ineffective as to such state, without modifying the balance of the agreement (but if the conflicting provisions of state law can be waived, they are waived by the railroad).

The agreement may contain a prepayment clause, giving the railroad the right at its option to anticipate any and all installments of principal, in inverse order of maturity, by paying a premium of $\frac{1}{10}$ of one percent per annum for each six months by which the installment is anticipated;[5] or to anticipate any of the installments due in the first five years, in inverse order of maturity, by paying a premium of ½ of one percent per annum for the period by which each installment is prepaid;[6] or on any semiannual installment date to prepay without premium one or more of the next four succeeding installments;[7] or to prepay on the sixth annual installment date or any installment date thereafter, in inverse order of maturity, one or more annual installments, at premiums declining from 5 percent if prepaid at the first opportunity to one percent if prepaid on the date of the fourteenth annual installment;[8] or to prepay without premium any or all installments, in inverse order of maturity.[9] Such privileges of prepayment without penalty were common in agreements negotiated at times when money was so plentiful that the borrowers were able to drive hard bargains, and interest rates were so low as to make prepayment seem rather academic.

The prepayment provisions contrast with the almost universal absence of such options in equipment trust

[5] Louisville and Nashville Agreement, dated as of December 1, 1952, carrying 3¼ percent interest.

[6] Atlantic Coast Line supplemental agreement, dated as of May 1, 1956, carrying 3¾ percent interest on the installments due in the first five years; no prepayment privilege on the installments due in the last ten years, carrying 4 percent interest.

[7] Bangor and Aroostook agreement, dated as of February 1, 1954, carrying 3⅞ percent interest.

[8] Wilson and Co. agreement, dated as of September 1, 1956, carrying 4⅛ percent interest.

[9] Charleston and Western Carolina agreement, dated as of April 15, 1949, carrying 2¾ percent interest.

## Conditional Sale Contracts

agreements.[10] Another contrasting feature is the general practice, outlined in the seventh paragraph of this chapter, of advancing funds and starting the accrual of interest as, and only as, each group of equipment is delivered. This may necessitate rather complicated provision for such contingencies as delays in delivery or default in payment.

Since lenders have a natural and healthy distaste for indefinite commitments, it is generally provided that units of equipment which cannot, for any reason, be delivered by some specified deadline are to be excluded from the agreement, with corresponding reduction in the aggregate purchase price and the deferred installments. Generally it is provided that if the delay results from strikes, fires, accidents, or other causes beyond the builder's control the railroad remains liable for the purchase and must arrange other financing for the units when ultimately delivered.[11] It is sometimes provided that the lenders shall receive, in consideration of their commitment to make the investment as equipment is delivered, a commitment fee at some such rate as ½ of one percent per annum on each payment, for the period prior to the closing date.[12] The commitment fee may be covered in a supplemental agreement,[13] or more rarely provision may be made for de-

[10] See above, Chapter VI.

[11] Agreements mentioned in footnotes 4, 6, and 7 above.

[12] Agreement, dated as of the first day of March, 1956, by and between General Motors Corporation . . . and Southern Pacific Company. St. Louis–San Francisco agreements dated as of January 1, 1957, specify a commitment fee at the rate of 1 percent per annum.

[13] Paragraph 6 of the agreement among The First National City Bank of New York and the lenders involved in the Atlantic Coast

positing the full amount of the deferred installments with the lenders' agent, for temporary investment in United States government securities, with the railroad obligated to pay interest at the full rate from date of deposit rather than from the dates the equipment is delivered and funds are applied to payment therefor.[14]

In the event of the railroad's default, which means continued and uncorrected failure to make the stipulated payments or carry out other provisions of the agreement, or proceedings in bankruptcy, reorganization, or insolvency, the builder's remedies are similar to those under an equipment trust agreement.[15] The builder at its option may declare the entire debt due and payable, may repossess the equipment wherever it may be found (the railroad being obligated to assemble the equipment and provide storage facilities for it), may sell the equipment at public or private sale (with or without assembling it at the point of sale) or may lease same, applying the proceeds of any sale or lease (after necessary costs and expenses) to payment of principal and interest.[16] It is expressly stipulated that no such repossession, lease, or sale is to terminate the railroad's obligation until the principal has

---

Line financing mentioned in note 5 above concerns commitment fees pursuant to a Commitment Letter dated May 1, 1956.

[14] Letter of Louisville and Nashville Railroad Company to Guaranty Trust Company of New York, under date of January 8, 1953, in connection with the financing mentioned in note 4 above.

[15] See Chapter VI, above.

[16] Some of the agreements are explicit in stating, what must necessarily be true in any case, that these remedies are subject to any mandatory legal requirements; e.g., agreements mentioned in footnotes 2, 6, 7, and 11 above.

## Conditional Sale Contracts

been paid in full, with interest to date of payment; that the remedies shall be cumulative rather than exclusive, and in addition to any other remedies existing at law or in equity; and that no delay or omission in the exercise of any power or remedy, or renewal or extension of any payment due, shall impair such power or remedy, or constitute a waiver of any default.

As the builder is not willing—generally cannot afford —to wait years for his payment, he assigns the conditional sale agreement to a lender, or an agent for several lenders, willing to make an investment on the terms stipulated in the agreement. The lender or lenders make payment to the builder, as each group of equipment is delivered, in an amount equal to the principal of the deferred installments, and take over the builder's right to receive from the railroad the deferred installments with interest and substantially all other rights under the agreement. The assignment stipulates that it does not cover the right to build the equipment and to receive that part of the purchase price in excess of the deferred payments (i.e., any down payment, and any excess of final price over the figure the lenders have agreed to finance), and is without prejudice to the builder's rights under the railroad's agreement to indemnify it against claims arising from accidents, taxes, and patents. The assignment is stated to be without recourse; i.e., the builder is to have no liability for the railroad's performance of its obligation, the lenders looking solely to the railroad and the equipment for their security.

The assignment warrants title to the equipment and

repeats the builder's undertaking to construct and deliver the equipment in accordance with the terms of the conditional sale agreement. It undertakes to indemnify the assignee against all expense, loss, or damage from any defense or counterclaim of the railroad against the builder, under his construction warranty or patent indemnity or otherwise, repeating the conditional sale agreement provision that any such claims are to be enforceable only against the builder and not against assignees, present or future. It likewise indemnifies the assignee against patent claims, other than on items specified by the railroad. If the conditional sale agreement has provided for marking the equipment, the assignment contains the builder's agreement that each unit, on delivery, will be plainly, permanently, and conspicuously marked to show the assignee's ownership.

The assignment contains the usual provision covering construction of the agreement under the laws of a specified state, and its execution in counterparts, and specifies that the assignee may in turn effectively assign any or all of its rights.

The assignment spells out, in somewhat more detail than the conditional sale agreement, the procedure at each "closing," listing the documents to be furnished (e.g., bill of sale from builder to assignee, transferring and warranting title to the equipment involved; certificate of the railroad's agent covering inspection and acceptance of the equipment and certifying to its marking; duplicate invoices endorsed with the railroad's certification of the correctness of unit prices and the builder's

## Conditional Sale Contracts

certification of the railroad's cash payment of any amount due from it; opinion of assignee's counsel as to validity and effect of the conditional sale agreement and the assignment, title to the equipment, and no necessity of approval from Interstate Commerce Commission or other governmental authority; opinion of builder's counsel and railroad's counsel on the same subjects, so far as their respective companies are concerned), and specifying that the obligation of the assignee (if acting as agent) to make payment is expressly conditioned upon prior receipt of funds from the lenders. In the event of default by any lender, the railroad may pay the defaulting share to the agent and its indebtedness will be proportionately reduced, but it shall not thereby acquire any rights under the assignment.[17]

Just as the conditional sale agreement establishes the underlying relationship between railroad and builder, conveying use and possession to the former while reserving title to the latter, and the assignment in turn conveys title, and right to receive payments, to the lender (or agent of several lenders), so the agency agreement covers the relation between the lenders and the bank which is acting as their agent.

The agent undertakes to acquire, pursuant to the assignment, the rights of the builder under the conditional sale agreement and to hold same and title to the equipment for the benefit of the lenders in proportion to their

[17] Agreement and Assignment, dated as of February 1, 1954, by and between American Car and Foundry Company . . . and Guaranty Trust Company of New York, paragraph 6.

respective interests in the loan. It is expressly agreed that the obligations of the agent are only those set forth in the agreement.

Upon each delivery of equipment and receipt by the agent of the delivery papers (third paragraph above) the agent is to give each lender and its counsel one copy (or counterpart) of each such paper together with a statement of its share in the payment for that delivery; on the closing date each lender is to have payment of its share in the hands of the agent who is to make payment thereof to the builder.[18] In the event any lender shall fail to pay his share, the railroad, as previously mentioned, may pay that share and reduce its indebtedness proportionately, without relieving the defaulting lender of its liability.

The agent acknowledges these payments by issuing to each lender a certificate of interest which sets forth its interest in that amount in the conditional sale agreement, the assignment, and the right, title, and interest of the agent in and to the equipment, specifies the due date of the installment or installments in which the particular lender is investing, names the interest rate, and specifies that the agent is to make the payments only as received from

---

[18] Sometimes the agreement specifies that the agent is to call upon the lenders in a particular order, calling upon the second only when the sum due from the first has been fully paid, and so on down the line; e.g., Agreement dated as of January 1, 1957, by and among Mercantile Trust Company, as Agent . . . and the Lenders named [in connection with St. Louis–San Francisco Railway Company financing] and Agreement dated as of October 1, 1956, by and among The New York Trust Company, as Agent . . . , and the corporation and trusts named in Schedule A [in connection with Kansas City Southern Railway financing].

## Conditional Sale Contracts

the railroad. There is no attempt or intention to make these certificates negotiable, but each lender agrees to surrender its certificate upon full payment.

The agent undertakes to accept funds paid to it by the railroad pursuant to the conditional sale agreement and assignment and, so long as it does not know of any continuing default, to apply such funds to payment of interest and principal, the installments of principal being as shown in the agency agreement (some of the lenders having agreed to take earlier installments, others later installments, still others a share in several, perhaps all, maturities) and in the respective certificates of interest. The agent agrees to receive and disburse the commitment fee,[19] and to accept and apply as provided in the conditional sale agreement all sums paid by the railroad on account of damaged, lost, or destroyed equipment, with prompt notice to each lender.

In the event of default, the agent is promptly to notify each lender, and shall thereafter take such action as may be directed by holders of two thirds of the indebtedness, the lenders indemnifying the agent against liability and expense, including counsel fees.

The lenders agree not to transfer or assign their respective interests except upon the express condition that the transferee or assignee shall be bound by the terms of the agency agreement.

The agreement contains the usual stipulations concerning the laws under which it is to be construed, and its

[19] See notes 12 and 13 above, and the corresponding paragraph of text.

execution in any number of counterparts. The agent reserves the right to resign on not less than thirty days' notice and to designate a successor, unless a successor has been selected by holders of a majority of the indebtedness.[20]

Sometimes the agreement contains a representation by each of the lenders that it is acquiring its interest in the conditional sale indebtedness

for its own account for investment and not with a view to, or for sale in connection with, or with any present intention of distributing or selling the same, but subject, nevertheless, to any requirement of law that the disposition of its property shall at all times be within its control.[21]

At least one agreement adds the further proviso, which is presumably implied in any event:

[20] This description is based on the agreement among The New York Trust Company and twelve other lenders, dated as of March 1, 1956, covering a Southern Pacific loan. Unlike conditional sale agreements and assignments, which are necessarily on file at the office of the Interstate Commerce Commission in Washington, D.C. (or in the case of agreements prior to 1952, at the capitals of the respective states), these agency agreements are not matters of public record. The assignee may permit inspection, or supply a list of lenders, one of whom may be willing to accommodate the student in this respect. Any extensive financial library, as in universities having schools of business, should make a point of acquiring copies of typical agreements; the best time to do so would be on the announcement of the financing, before the extra copies (if any) have been discarded or given away. As the several documents are usually bound together in a single printing, the library which receives one will usually have the entire set.

[21] Agreement dated as of January 1, 1957, by and among Mercantile Trust Company, as Agent . . . and the Lenders named (in connection with St. Louis–San Francisco Railway Company financing).

## Conditional Sale Contracts

and subject also to the understanding that if any Lender should later decide to sell such Certificates, or the interests in the Conditional Sale Agreements evidenced thereby, or any portion thereof, this Agreement will not preclude its so doing.[22]

For prudential and statutory reasons, deferred installments rarely, if ever, cover a period longer than fifteen years. Within that period, however, conditional sale agreements show considerably more variety, in both maturity schedules and down payments, than do equipment trust agreements.

Twenty years ago, many railroads which had little credit and less cash found it possible to buy diesel-electric locomotives with little or no down payment through monthly installments over a period of five years. Initial diesel purchases, for use in switching and similar service where they offered the greatest economies, would pay for themselves within some such period; the rapid retirement of the debt speedily built up an equity which no receiver or bankruptcy trustee could afford to jeopardize; and monthly maturities both contributed to this rapid retirement and minimized the temptation to default on any one installment; there might be some real money involved in an annual or semiannual installment, whereas each monthly payment would seem too small to precipitate a crisis and the series of payments steadily reinforced the creditor's position.

Such a rate of payment was not one the railroads

[22] Agreement dated as of February 29, 1952, between The Philadelphia National Bank and other banks, insurance companies, and other lenders, relating to Conditional Sale Agreements of The Pennsylvania Railroad Company.

wanted to maintain, or could be expected to maintain on purchases less phenomenally profitably than the initial diesels. Most of the recent conditional sale agreements have called for serial payments over a fifteen-year period. Some have provided for substantially the down payment to be expected on equipment trust agreements.[23] Others have sought to provide a substitute for the down payment by increasing the earlier installments.[24] Still others permit substantially the full cost of the equipment to be paid in equal installments over the fifteen-year period, evidently in the belief that the credit of the borrower and the value of the equipment provide adequate protection without any down payment or acceleration of installments.[25]

Lenders rarely insist upon the specific assignment of a particular lot of equipment to each lender, rather than

[23] E.g., 18 percent in the Charleston & Western Carolina agreements dated as of April 15, 1949; and 20 percent in the Louisville and Nashville agreements dated as of December 1, 1952, and the Southern Pacific agreements dated as of March 1, 1956.

[24] E.g., the Bangor and Aroostook agreement dated as of February 1, 1954, makes each of the installments maturing in the first five years more than twice those maturing in the last ten years, so that the outstanding balance would be reduced to not more than 58.40 percent at the end of the fourth year, as compared with 58.67 percent at that time with the conventional 20 percent down payment (see Table 4, fifth figure in column 2).

Likewise the Pennsylvania Railroad agreements and assignments to the Philadelphia National Bank, dated as of March 1, 1952, provide for payment of half the loan in the first six years, thus reducing the outstanding balance to 50 percent at the start of the seventh year, as compared with 48 percent at that time with the conventional 20 percent down payment (see Table 4, column 2).

[25] E.g., Kansas City Southern agreement dated as of October 1, 1956; Wilson & Co., Inc., agreement dated as of September 1, 1956; Atlantic Coast Line supplemental agreement dated as of May 1, 1956.

## Conditional Sale Contracts

assignment of the entire lot to a single representative of all the lenders.[26] Such a course multiplies the number of agreements and assignments, although it may slightly simplify the drafting of each, and is not considered to add to the security; in fact most investors and attorneys would probably agree with Stevenson's comment that

it is better for an investor to have, say, a 5% interest in 1,000 boxcars than a separate conditional sale contract covering 50 boxcars. If the railroad were in bankruptcy, it might be willing to abrogate a conditional sale contract relating to 50 boxcars, but it certainly would give a great deal more thought to abrogating a contract involving 1,000 boxcars.[27]

[26] E.g., Charleston & Western Carolina agreements dated as of April 15, 1949.

[27] John Stevenson, "Financing of Railroad Equipment," *The Analysts Journal*, IX (No. 5, November, 1953), 29.

A further advantage of assignment to a single representative of all the lenders is that it eliminates any necessity of remarking the equipment in the event one lender should resell his interest; marking 50 boxcars, which might be scattered all over the country, would be an expensive and tedious process which might block any resale of the contract.

*CHAPTER VIII*

# Lease Arrangements

THIS chapter concerns bona fide leases, as opposed to conditional sale agreements and the Philadelphia Plan leases, which are in effect disguised conditional sales. The essential point of these true leases is that they do not contemplate acquisition of the property by the railroad at the end of the lease, containing neither a provision for automatic transfer of title to the lessee on completion of payments nor an option for the lessee to purchase.

The best-known of these lease plans is that announced by The Equitable Life Assurance Society in 1949. Equitable simultaneously enters into a manufacturing agreement with a builder of locomotives or freight cars, by which it undertakes to pay 80 percent or 90 percent of the cost of the equipment upon its delivery and the balance over a short period of years (e.g., 20 equal consecutive quarterly installments, with interest from date of delivery), and a lease to a responsible railroad, by which the latter undertakes to pay for the equipment a fixed rental calculated to pay the debt to the builder as scheduled, and to retire Equitable's investment over the fifteen-year period of the lease, together with a satisfactory return on the investment.

## Lease Arrangements

In the event of default under the lease, Equitable is not obligated to continue payments to the builder during the period of default. The builder has no lien upon the equipment but in effect has an option to repurchase it in such an event at the amount of Equitable's net investment; i.e., Equitable cannot terminate its obligation to the builder without giving him such an opportunity.

The builder agrees to indemnify Equitable against patent claims, and warrants the equipment to comply with the specifications of the manufacturing agreement, with any applicable rules of interchange of the Association of American Railroads, and with all governmental laws, rules, regulations, and requirements. It likewise agrees to pay Equitable's counsel fees and expenses in connection with the agreement and lease. Delivery of the equipment is to be made to the lessee, for account of Equitable, and the latter is to make payment as outlined above on acceptance by the lessee and receipt of the usual documents —bill of sale, invoice, certificates of inspection, delivery and acceptance (including proof of marking as provided in the lease), and opinions of counsel, including those on adequacy of filing with Interstate Commerce Commission and freedom from any requirement of governmental approval for the lease.

The lease provides for inspection and acceptance of the equipment, its permanent and conspicuous marking to show Equitable's ownership, and payment of a fixed rental, at monthly or quarterly intervals, in amounts decreasing each three years. Lessee agrees to pay promptly, or reimburse Equitable for, all taxes other than income taxes; to pay the net discounted value of remaining rentals plus net scrap value of any unit lost, destroyed, or damaged beyond repair (and in some cases to insure each unit in amount at least sufficient to cover this sum); to maintain and repair the equipment and comply with all governmental laws, regulations, and requirements, and the interchange rules where applicable; to furnish Equitable each January, and oftener if requested, an accurate inventory of the equipment with evidence of its continued marking; to see to the filing of the lease with the Interstate Commerce Commission, and elsewhere if and when necessary; and to indemnify Equitable against all claims, expense, and liability arising out of the use or operation of the equipment or any accident in which it may be involved. Equitable makes no warranty as to condition, quality, or suitability of the equipment.

Lessee is to have the right and option of renewing the lease, for a stipulated additional period of years, at a specified reduced rental, with the privilege of terminating the extended lease as to any unit on thirty days' notice, and is to make settlement by payment of its net scrap value for any unit lost, destroyed, or damaged beyond repair. Upon expiration of the original or extended term of the lease, lessee is to deliver equipment to Equitable, or upon Equitable's order, at its own expense at such point on its own lines or to such connecting carrier as Equitable shall designate, and shall provide up to 100 days' free storage for same; this provision is stated to be of the essence of the lease, and enforceable by court order, and the lessee (without in any way limiting its obligations) irrevocably appoints Equitable agent and attorney with full authority to reclaim any unit from whoever may be in possession of it. Equitable may assign the lease without consent of the lessee, but the latter may not assign it without consent of Equitable, or permit any units to pass out of its control except in the normal interchange of traffic.

In the event of default, which means continued and uncorrected failure to make the specified rental payments or carry out its other obligations, or proceedings in bankruptcy or reorganization, Equitable may at its option take court action to enforce the lease or recover damages, or may terminate the lease (without terminating the lessee's liability) and repossess the equipment, with the right to recover rentals to date of repossession, together with the discounted value of rentals for the balance of the original term of the lease (stated to be damages for loss of a bargain rather than a penalty) and any other damages sustained. The remedies are stated to be cumulative rather than exclusive, and in addition to any other remedies existing at law or in equity, and the lessee waives (so far as it legally can) any legal requirements which might limit or modify any of these remedies.[1]

Another leasing plan is that sponsored by National Equipment Leasing Corporation, which was formed by

[1] The leases, but not the manufacturing agreements, are necessarily matters of public record, on file with the Interstate Commerce Commission in Washington (or in the case of those prior to 1952 at state capitals). This description is based on a specimen furnished by Mr. Hunter Holding, Second Vice President of the Equitable Life Assurance Society.

Pittsburgh interests for the purpose of supplying capital goods to industry for periods which normally extend through the estimated useful life of the equipment, on the basis of rental payments for the right to use the equipment. National states that

> Under present conditions of high taxes, high replacement costs and increased operating charges in general, it is becoming increasingly difficult for companies to accumulate from earnings the capital necessary to expand and modernize production facilities. As a solution, more and more companies are turning to the idea of leasing.
> . . . In many industries where purchase has long been taken for granted, arrangements are being made to lease virtually every type of equipment, from airplanes to mining machinery, from typewriters to rolling mills, from automotive equipment to machine tools, from locomotives to ships.
> . . . *use* of equipment produces profit, not ownership, and that it may be better to pay for *use* out of current income than pay for ownership out of past profit.
> . . . A true lease conveys *only the right of use,* subject to specified payments; and any agreement which, by its wording or terms, suggests that it does not preserve a true lessee-lessor relationship is likely to be challenged. Legitimate tax advantage *may be* obtained through leasing, but the nature of the agreement, not its title, must be the basis of obtaining these benefits.[2]

Unlike Equitable, which from the nature of the life insurance business has vast accumulations of capital and faces primarily the problem of how profitable railway

---

[2] Brochure, *When Does It Pay to LEASE Equipment?,* published by National Equipment Leasing Corporation, Pittsburgh, Pennsylvania, pp. 1, 2, 4.

equipment leases may be in comparison with such alternative investments as real estate, mortgages, or government and corporate securities, National must seek outside financing. This it obtains by trusteeing the leases for the benefit of institutional investors, which "meets the legal test of preserving the true lessor-lessee relationship and . . . permits the participation of a large number of sources of capital, enabling National to acquire and lease property of almost unlimited initial cost." [3]

In general, National's deals involve four essential agreements.[4] The Manufacturing Agreement covers the construction of the locomotives to the specifications of the lessee and their sale to National for cash on the closing date, the railroad using the locomotives on temporary lease from the builder until the closing date.

The Lease, which creates and defines the railroad's rights and obligations and the owner's remedies, is substantially similar in terms to the Equitable leases outlined in the fifth, sixth, and seventh paragraphs of this chapter.

The Trust Agreement and Assignment transfers the lease and title to the locomotives to a trustee for the benefit of the investors, and defines the rights and duties of the trustee. It sets forth a form of trust certificates which,

[3] *Ibid.*, p. 8.

[4] This description is based on the financing announced in The New York *Times,* April 16, 1957, covering the lease of diesel-electric locomotives costing $13,903,888 to The Baltimore and Ohio Railroad Company and private sale to institutional investors of participations to that amount; lease and trust agreement recorded with Interstate Commerce Commission in Washington on August 15, 1957.

unlike the certificates of interest in conditional sale agreements,[5] are specifically stated to be transferable upon the books of the trustee, who upon such transfer will issue a new certificate to the transferee; it stipulates that the registered holder may be treated as absolute owner of the certificate, notwithstanding any notice to the contrary. Provision is made for replacing, on proper evidence and indemnity, any certificate mutilated, destroyed, lost, or stolen.

National undertakes to have the locomotives marked to show its interest as owner and the trustee's as assignee; agrees that in the event of default the trustee may exercise any or all of the owner's remedies under the lease, and irrevocably appoints the trustee agent and attorney with full power and authority to execute such instruments as may be appropriate in that connection; and agrees to indemnify the trustee against all claims arising out of the ownership or use of the locomotives.

The trustee accepts the trust and agrees, so far as reasonably possible, to enforce the railroad's performance of the lease. It agrees to accept all payments of rental and distribute them pro rata among the holders of trust certificates; to administer the insurance funds or other payments for locomotives stolen, destroyed, or damaged; to notify the certificate holders of any default and act upon instructions of a majority, reserving the right to require indemnity for any advances or expenses. It acknowledges receipt from National of compensation for its normal services over the full term of the trust,

[5] See above, Chapter VII.

## Lease Arrangements

and reserves the right to resign and turn over the trust to a qualified successor. On completion of agreed payments, including interest on any delayed payments, the trust is to terminate and title to the locomotives is to revert to National.

The Purchase Agreement presumably covers the undertaking of the participating investors to buy from National the rentals to be paid over the terms of the lease, the purchases being represented by delivery of the trust certificates, and spells out in the usual detail the closing procedure, commitment fee, and representations of the several parties.[6]

Alco Products (formerly American Locomotive Company)[7] and General Motors[8] have recently formed subsidiaries to lease diesels to railroads which cannot, or will not, finance their acquisition through equipment trusts or conditional sale agreements. The formula is approximately that just described in connection with National Equipment Leasing Corporation—not a disguised conditional sale, but a true lease, financed by assignment of lease, title, and payments to the institutional investors who are providing the funds. The flexibility of the plan is such that if and when necessary the seller can add his

[6] As in the case of conditional sale agreements, discussed in Chapter VII, above.

[7] Lease and agreement, between Alco Products Inc. and Pennsylvania Railroad, and assignments to American Locomotive and Equipment Company (subsidiary) and to Guaranty Trust Company of New York as agent, recorded with Interstate Commerce Commission in Washington on November 18, 1957, and November 21, 1957, respectively.

[8] *The Wall Street Journal*, December 30, 1957.

endorsement of part or all of the payments; in other words, the investor who is unwilling to finance the entire cost by an assignment "without recourse," under which he can only look to the railroad and the equipment for security, may get, as a substitute for the down payment which is almost universal under equipment trust agreements [9] and sometimes available in conditional sale contracts,[10] a guaranty in some agreed amount from the seller.

In July, 1957, Mr. James M. Symes, president of the Pennsylvania Railroad Company, presented before a subcommittee of the House of Representatives a proposal, incorporated into bills later introduced as HR2906 and S9597, for a Railway Equipment Agency to be owned and financed by the federal government, with $500,000-000 initial capital and authority to borrow four times that amount, making a total of $2,500,000,000. This sum would be used to buy rolling stock for lease to the railroads over agreed periods, perhaps fifteen years for diesels, twenty for freight cars, and ten for passenger cars, at net rentals sufficient to cover cost less scrap value together with interest at a rate one quarter of one percent above that paid by the agency on its borrowing, all repairs and maintenance to be at the expense of the leasing railroad. The rate would be the same for all roads, with allocations in the event of the agency being unable to supply the demand; the lessee might reasign its lease to another railroad, or the agency might lease to another

[9] See above, Chapter VI.
[10] See above, Chapter VII, footnote 23,

road equipment which it had repossessed in consequence of default, but in neither event would the lease extend beyond the terms initially fixed; at the end of that period the equipment must be sold at its fair value to the government for stock-piling with other strategic materials held for national defense purposes, or be scrapped.

Mr. Symes argued that the plan would be fully self-supporting, in contrast to the subsidies paid to other forms of transportation; that it would assure the country a railroad system in first-class condition, ready for any emergency, with adequate capacity; that it would give the government an opportunity to stockpile equipment against a war emergency at a relatively low cost; and that maintaining the physical condition of the railroads at a high level would be a stimulant to the peacetime economy, productive of additional income. For the railroads, he argued that the plan would enable them to put their entire plant in first-class condition without straining their credit, releasing funds from the equipment budget for modernization of yards, signal control, and roadway improvement; to operate more efficiently in consequence, keeping down transportation costs and increasing earnings; to insure their participation in the expanding economy; to reduce the over-all cost of equipment through standardization which, with increased purchases on a more regular basis, would permit the suppliers to put their output on a mass-production basis; to interest the government in the welfare of the railroads through its financial stake in the leases; to establish the principle of the user's paying full cost for services rendered; and to avoid the loss of residual value which is involved in private leasing plans.[11]

The plan was presented on behalf of the eastern roads, Mr. Symes explaining in answer to a question that the western and southern roads "seem to think they can get their own money." The endorsement of the eastern roads appears to have been somewhat less than enthusiastic; although Delaware Lackawanna and Western is the only one specifically disowning the plan, there seems to be a feeling among many railroad men and railroad investors that this might prove a fatal step toward government ownership. Opinion is divided between those who think that the proposals could not be supported by anyone who remembers the problems which government financing presented in the reorganizations of the last decade, and those who hold the view that present financing choices are limited to "entirely inadequate" earnings and depreciation, or "impossible" borrowing, so that a breakdown of transportation service may prove a more serious inducement than any other to government ownership. There was obviously no time to act on the plan proposed before adjournment of Congress in September, 1957, nor was it incorporated into the Transportation Act of 1958.[12] With what success the plan may be promoted at future sessions remains to be seen.

[11] See *Traffic World*, July 27, 1957; less detailed accounts in *Railway Age*, July 29, 1957; The New York *Times*, The New York *Herald-Tribune*, and *Wall Street Journal*, July 25, 1957.

[12] 72 *Stat.* 568.

*CHAPTER IX*

# Marketing Equipment Obligations

SINCE 1928 the Interstate Commerce Commission has required competitive bidding on railroad sales of equipment trust certificates.[1] The railroad announces by advertisement its intention of opening sealed bids at a stated time and place, for a designated amount of certificates, maturing in stated annual (or semiannual) installments, to be issued under the Philadelphia Plan against the equipment described, subject to the approval of counsel and the authorization of the Interstate Commerce Commission. The invitation to bidders, by circular directed to leading financial institutions and all who may have answered the advertisement, sets forth all the necessary information and stipulates that each bid is to name a dividend [2] rate, in some multiple of one eighth percent, and a price, not less than 99 percent, for certificates bearing that rate. The award is ordinarily to the bidder whose proposal represents the lowest net interest cost to the railroad, although the latter reserves the right to reject any and all bids.[3] All the documents are filed with the Interstate Commerce Commission prior to the bidding,

[1] See above, Chapter IV.

[2] I.e., interest; see above, Chapter VI, third paragraph.

[3] The New York Central rejected all bids for a proposed issue of $6,450,000 equipment trust certificates on June 11, 1957.

but the sale is made subject to its authorization, as price and dividend must be covered by supplemental filing subsequent to the bidding.

While the invitation goes to all prospective bidders—banks and institutional investors, as well as dealers—the actual bidding is mostly by dealers, and in recent years nearly every issue has been bought by syndicates headed either by Halsey Stuart & Co. Inc. or by Salomon Bros. & Hutzler. Such syndicates bought all of the 63 issues sold in the first nine months of 1957; all but one of the 64 sold in 1956, 30 of 35 in 1955, 32 of 39 in 1954, and 45 of 52 in 1953.

Each syndicate is legally a separate venture, formed on the invitation of its leader to bid for a particular issue with a view to its prompt resale to investors if the bid is successful. The price is set by agreement at a meeting immediately before the bidding, at which each member has the opportunity of withdrawing if dissatisfied. In fixing on a bid price the members must first determine the figure at which they are willing to undertake the sale of each maturity, then total these figures to determine the aggregate proceeds of the entire issue, and somewhere below that total decide upon a bid which is judged high enough to win the award and at the same time low enough to provide an adequate margin for expense, risk, and profit. The membership of successive syndicates under the same leadership shows considerable stability; i.e., Halsey's invitations go to one list and Salomon's to another, and the same firms accept one invitation after another on the basis of past favorable experience and per-

## Marketing Equipment Obligations

haps a suspicion that too many rejections might eliminate future invitations. Each member of the syndicate shares the profit or loss on the deal; he may be liable for any unsold certificates, in proportion to his subscription, or the agreement may provide for reducing each member's liability by the amount of his own sales, so that the member who has sold his full quota has no liability in connection with any unsold balance. In either case the total of subscriptions, including the leader's, adds up to the amount of the issue.

Delivery and payment is ordinarily scheduled for a date a few weeks subsequent to the bidding, by which time it is expected that all the certificates will be resold, so that the syndicate will not have to put up any money if successful; on the other hand it might, if it has priced the certificates too high, have to take up the entire issue. The syndicate ordinarily tries to set the resale prices so that all the certificates can be resold without much delay, to avoid tying up its capital and to reduce the market risk. If the certificates can in fact be resold immediately after the bidding, the syndicate has no worry about subsequent developments, but may find that it has done the business at an unnecessarily small margin and missed a good opportunity to add to its salable inventory. On the other hand, to the extent that the certificates remain unsold the syndicate is taking the risk of possible adverse developments, political or economic, so that too high a price, whether from misjudging the current market or speculating on an improvement, may mean not merely an unprofitable deal but a substantial risk.

The potential profit is measured by the gross spread, the difference between the aggregate selling price, at the advertised prices, and the cost of the certificates—what a merchant would call the markup on his wholesale purchase. From this spread must be paid any expenses, such as advertising, postage, insurance, and concessions—i.e., commissions or discounts—to dealers who are not in the syndicate. These latter are naturally small, the most common scale being "0–⅛"—i.e., nothing on the shorter maturities, and one eighth of one percent [4] on the longer; less frequently "0–⅛–¼," meaning one eighth of one percent on the middle maturities and one fourth of one percent on the longer; in an extreme case, with an unusually wide gross spread, such a figure as "¼–½."

The gross spread rarely amounts to one percent or more; on only four of the 46 issues in the first six months of 1957, seven of the 62 on which data are available in 1956,[5] none in 1955, one of 35 in 1954, four of 51 in 1953. The median spread on the 1957 issues was 0.65 percent, on the 1956 issues 0.70 percent, on 1955 issues 0.54 percent, on 1954 issues 0.57 percent, and on 1953 issues 0.69 percent. These spreads reflect the tendency of margins to narrow in periods of easy money; 1954 was conspicuously such a year, the net interest cost of the financing exceeding 3 percent on only five of the

[4] All quotations are based on the principal amount of the certificates.

[5] Data are not available when all or a large part of the issue is placed privately—i.e., not reoffered for public sale. These figures were compiled by the writer from *Corporate Financing Directory*, published semiannually by Investment Dealers Digest, New York.

## Marketing Equipment Obligations

issues, in sharp contrast with 1953 when only two issues were financed at less than 3 percent, or 1956–57 when none of the financing cost less than 3 percent and a large part cost more than 4 percent.

Anything which can be expected to influence the sale of the certificates appears to be reflected even more conspicuously in the spread, which represents the underwriters' judgment on the cost and risk involved in distribution,[6] than in the net interest cost. Working on the basis of individual issues rather than on that of the averages used in the preceding paragraph, we find that lower interest costs are generally (though not invariably) accompanied by lower spreads and vice versa, but that the variation in spread substantially exceeds that in interest cost. Of the financing in the second half of 1956, for instance, the lowest cost was the New York, Chicago and St. Louis Second Equipment Trust of 1956, sold July 11 at a net interest rate of 3.41 percent, and the highest was the New York, New Haven and Hartford Equipment Trust of 1956 #2, sold October 16 at 5.32 percent; the interest cost on the latter was about half again as much as on the former, but the spread was 1.548 percent as compared with 0.478 percent, or more than three times as great. Both were fifteen-year issues secured by new diesel-electric locomotives with 20 percent down payment, so the difference in rating (Aa on the New York, Chicago and St. Louis, and Baa, which is two groups lower, on the New Haven) reflects the difference in the credit of the borrowers, based on such factors as their history,

[6] I.e., resale of the issue to investors.

earning power, traffic, present financial position, and policies. This difference in credit and rating is in turn reflected, together with such factors as the state of the market at the respective dates, experience with previous issues and any knowledge of their present distribution, and the opinions, prejudices, and policies of prospective buyers, in the interest cost and the spread.

A better comparison might be issues of different quality offered at practically the same date. The difference of two rating groups between Burlington and North Western equipments, both sold November 8, 1956, is reflected in interest costs of 3.97 percent and 5.18 percent, and spreads of 0.65 percent and 1.30 percent—in other words, North Western had to pay about one third more for its borrowing but the spread was twice as great. Similarly New Haven on October 16 had an interest cost of 5.32 percent, or about one third higher than that of Reading on certificates sold at 4.10 percent the next day, but the spread was more than twice as great—1.548 percent vs. 0.75 percent. On May 29 North Western paid 4.46 percent on its borrowing against 3.37 percent for Denver and Rio Grande, again a differential of one third, but the spread was two and one-half times as great—1.50 percent against 0.60 percent. On February 1 North Western paid 3.87 percent against 3.11 percent on borrowing by Chesapeake and Ohio the following day, a differential of about one quarter, but the spread of 0.86 percent was more than twice Chesapeake's 0.425 percent.

The highest spread reported on any of these issues was 2.50 percent on the initial Boston and Maine financing

## Marketing Equipment Obligations

on February 28, 1956. This, like the 4.60 percent interest —at a time when no one else had paid even 4 percent for several years past or would for several months to come— reflected the underwriters' apprehensions as to investor reception of the name in view of the well publicized troubles of the road—recent financial readjustment, commutation and terminal problems, automotive competition, and a major maturity to meet in 1960. The road sold an additional issue on similar terms, 4.54 percent interest and 1.19 percent spread, on June 19, and a third, at 6.11 percent interest and 2.32 percent spread, on January 28, 1957.

These figures illustrate the importance of the borrower's credit. Equipment trust certificates may be the cheapest financing vehicle, perhaps the only one available to the road whose credit is not of the best, and their legal status,[7] together with experience in three quarters of a century of receivership and reorganization proceedings,[8] demonstrates that they are likely to be the best protected of the road's obligations, but they are by no means riskless investments. Even when so well secured, by an adequate equity in modern and indispensable equipment, as to be virtually certain of eventual payment, they face the possibility of litigation and delays in the event of reorganization proceedings, actual or threatened, and the probability of finding few, if any, buyers during the period of uncertainty; in other words, the investor who buys a particular maturity in order to assure himself of funds at that particular date must look to the credit of the

[7] See above, Chapter IV.   [8] See above, Chapter V.

railroad and its probability of avoiding trouble, rather than to the security which may assure his getting out whole in the long run but can hardly assure prompt payment, or an adequate market in the event of actual or threatened delay.

The market for equipment trust certificates is largely among institutional investors—life insurance companies, savings banks, trustees, and others—to whom income taxes are not an important problem. Even the yields available in 1957, greatly as they exceeded those of years prior to 1956, were hardly attractive to individuals to whom the return would be reduced by one fifth to nine tenths, depending on their income tax bracket. The efforts of the underwriting syndicate are directed at such institutional investors, many of whom have been lined up prior to the bidding and have pretty well made up their minds at what price (if any) they would be interested in the issue. The higher grade issues may be pretty well sold by telephone within a few hours of the bidding, if the underwriters have gauged their market correctly; the wider spreads on the less salable issues are to compensate for the sales effort and expense necessary in such cases, together with the risk of finding the certificates unsalable, especially in the event of adverse developments during the time that must necessarily be allowed for finding, and convincing, buyers.

Reference has already been made [9] to the possibility of placing privately—i.e., not reoffering for public sale—part or all of the issue. To the extent that underwriters

[9] See above, footnote 5.

## Marketing Equipment Obligations

can arrange this prior to the bidding, they eliminate the underwriting risk, in effect acting as agents for the investor. When we read that the First National Bank of Dallas bought $960,000 Texas-New Mexico Railway Equipment 2 ¾s on April 15, 1953, and $1,240,000 Texas and Pacific Railway Equipment 2s on March 24, 1954, with no reoffering in either case, the assumption is that the bank was either buying for its own investment or, more likely, making part or all of the purchase as agent for its customers; in fact, we really know that this is the case, since banks are no longer permitted to deal, as underwriters, in corporate securities for resale.[10] Likewise, when one of the dealers places privately several maturities of an issue [11] or the entire issue [12] we can assume that in respect to those it is acting not as principal but as agent. In so acting, it need charge only a nominal service fee, since it is incurring no liability; the advantage to the dealer lies in making this modest fee without risk, and to the investor in increasing the probability of getting the certificates at the price he is willing to pay, since the dealer can increase his bid to the railroad by the difference between this fee and the spread that would be necessary to cover the risk of a bid for resale.

Such private placement is the customary means of selling obligations which do not require the approval of the

[10] Banking Act of 1935.

[11] Blair, Rollins and Company on July 7, 1954; Pressprich and Company on January 19, 1955, and October 5, 1954; Salomon on April 28, 1955, and April 4, 1956; Halsey on June 20, 1955; and Kidder, Peabody and Company on June 15, 1955.

[12] Salomon on October 4, 1956.

Interstate Commerce Commission—i.e., conditional sale contracts of railroads, and both conditional sale contracts and equipment trust certificates of private car lines. A public offering of such obligations would require registration with the Securities and Exchange Commission under the Securities Act of 1933, from which obligations approved by the Interstate Commerce Commission under Section 20a of the Interstate Commerce Act are exempt.[13] To avoid the very substantial expense and delay of such registration, the sales are so negotiated as not to constitute a public offering, within the terms of the Securities Act and the Securities and Exchange Commission regulations. The issuer negotiates, directly or through commercial bankers or investment dealers (generally the latter) with a limited number of institutional investors, taking care to avoid anything that might be construed as a public offering and not to "use up names" unnecessarily—i.e., not to make an offering to or solicit a bid from investors who are not really interested. From his daily contact with the market, the dealer has a pretty good idea who is likely to be interested in the issue, and how to place it with a limited number of such investors without anything in the nature of a general solicitation. This knowledge of markets and techniques generally makes it worthwhile for the issuer to employ a dealer rather than attempt to do the job himself. The dealer expects a reasonable compensation, presumably somewhat less than the spread on an underwriting, since in this case he is acting as agent without a financial commitment.

[13] See above, Chapter IV, next to last paragraph.

## Marketing Equipment Obligations

Whether the financing is public or private, the managers naturally try to sell each maturity to the investors who will find it most useful, and can therefore be expected to pay most for it—e.g., the shorter maturities to commercial banks and the longer to those, such as pension trusts and insurance companies, whose interest is in income and intrinsic strength rather than in early repayment. The pricing reflects the demands of these several groups. When interest rates are low and there is a surplus of bank funds available, as for some years before and after the Second World War, we are likely to have "a steep interest curve"; i.e., short-term rates are likely to be well below longer term, even for obligations of the same borrower—e.g., the United States government. During the war, for instance, the rate on ninety-one-day United States Treasury bills was $\frac{3}{8}$ percent, on one year Treasury certificates $\frac{7}{8}$ percent, on Treasury notes maturing within five years $1\frac{1}{2}$ percent, increasing beyond that point to $2\frac{1}{2}$ percent on the longest bonds. Under such circumstances the yield on the initial maturities was extremely low, scaling up to a maximum on the last maturity. Consider the Bessemer and Lake Erie Equipment Trust of 1940, for instance—probably the lowest cost issue of all time—and scaled from 0.20 percent on the initial maturity and 0.80 percent on the fifth year to 1.50 percent on the tenth and last year. As recently as January 5, 1955, an issue of Southern Pacific equipment trust certificates was priced to yield 1.50 percent for the one year maturity, 2.45 percent for five years, 2.80 percent for ten years, and 2.90 percent for fifteen years.

Two years later, rising interest rates and tight money had completely changed the pattern, producing a curve which was almost flat. From the middle of 1956 until late in 1957 the yield on United States government securities maturing in from three to five years exceeded that on longer term government bonds.[14] Consequently, most of the equipment issues offered during the period were so priced as to show little or no difference in yields on maturities beyond the first few years; the usual scale was a small differential—say 0.25 percent to 0.50 percent lower yield—on the initial maturities, with a level scale from about the fifth year.[15]

What of secondary markets, the marketability of equipment obligations subsequent to the original distribution? Can the purchaser count on resale at will, or is he locked into his investment until its maturity?

In a sense, each maturity of each issue is *sui generis;* the certificates may be similar to those of other maturities of the same issue, or of like maturities in other issues of the same road, or of another road, but they are identical and interchangeable only within the same maturity of the particular issue. Thus the $2,539 million equipment obligations outstanding at the end of 1955,[16] or even the $1,546 million equipment trust certificates [17] which make

[14] *Federal Reserve Chart Book on Financial and Business Statistics, January, 1958* (Washington, Board of Governors of the Federal Reserve System), p. 22.

[15] The writer's computation from data supplied by Salomon Bros. & Hutzler. Seven of the nine issues publicly offered in May, 1956, and four of five in the following month had perfectly level scales—i.e., the same yield for all maturities.

[16] See above, Table 3.

[17] *Statistics of Railways* (1955), Table 141.

## Marketing Equipment Obligations

up the greater part of that total, do not have a single market, like the $2,609 million United States of America Treasury 4 percent Notes due August 1, 1961, or the 278 million shares of General Motors common stock, but rather a whole group of closely related markets, like those for serial bonds of neighboring municipalities. The holder cannot count on an immediate bid "on the wire," as with government obligations or active stocks, any more than he could count on the dealer to supply on demand certificates of a particular maturity in a named issue. Unless the dealer wishes to buy "for stock," he will need time to find a buyer interested in that particular item. Ordinarily this does not require much time, and the certificates are probably as marketable as any corporate obligations, with their serial maturity contributing intrinsic strength and an element of stability lacking in longer term bonds, but the holder is deluding himself if he thinks of them as a liquid resource in the same sense as short governments. They can generally be considered a good secondary reserve—necessarily secondary, from the standpoint of intrinsic strength and more particularly that of liquidity, to governments of similar maturity.

What of the obligations which have been privately placed? The registration provisions of the Securities Act apply only to the issuer and to those controlled by, controlling, or under common control with the issuer, or buying from him with a view to resale.[18] The bona fide in-

[18] The Securities Act, discussed briefly above in Chapter IV, is 15 U.S.C. Section 77; the conclusion expressed in this sentence is drawn from the exemptions in 77d, read in connection with the definitions in other paragraphs.

vestor who subsequently decides to resell is at liberty to do so publicly or privately, without restrictions beyond the common ones of honesty and fair dealing. The burden of proof may be on him to demonstrate that the original purchase was in fact for investment and not with a view to future resale, but he is by no means locked into the investment if he should decide to sell and can obtain a satisfactory bid.

The dealers will accommodate him in finding such a bid, just as they would in the case of equipment trust certificates originally offered through competitive bidding. The private car line certificates, issued in negotiable form in $1,000 denomination with all the machinery of dividend warrants and independent trustee, enjoy a good resale market as long as the credit of the issuer remains satisfactory. Conditional sale contracts, not being technically negotiable or issued in small denominations, present a somewhat different problem. They must be acquired by assignment rather than by endorsement and delivery, and because the assignee's position differs legally from that of the "holder in due course" of a negotiable instrument, the purchaser may think it necessary to have his attorney review the transaction in somewhat more detail than in buying a negotiable security in the open market. However sales can be and are negotiated, dealers jumping at the opportunity to arrange the transfer of such contracts, in blocks large enough to be worth the trouble, from one institutional investor to another.[19]

[19] But see Chapter VII, footnote 27, for comment on the obstacle which may be presented by remarking the equipment in certain cases.

*Marketing Equipment Obligations* 149

These comments, as to original placement and subsequent resale, would presumably apply equally to the assignments of interest in National Equipment Leasing Corporation leases described in Chapter VIII.

Maturity of the obligation and credit of the issuer were mentioned a few paragraphs above as distinguishing items affecting the market for each block of equipment trust certificates; the security of the issue is another. In Chapter VI [20] the effect of various down payment and maturity schedules was discussed at some length. To these should be added the nature of the equipment involved. Not only may one investor set more weight than another upon large down payment and/or rapid retirement, but he may also have decided opinions upon the desirability of various types of equipment. Few care for passenger cars, for instance; in fact, this is so generally recognized that certificates secured primarily by passenger cars are rarely offered for competitive bidding—only four in the four years 1953–56, if we define "primarily" to mean more than 50 percent.[21] Unless the credit of the road is superlative, the original distribution of such issues requires extra sales effort and a convincing presentation of the value and necessity of this particular equipment, and the resale market is likely to be somewhat limited. In the decade after the war some prospective purchasers shied away from issues secured by steam locomotives; today not all are sold on trailer-on-flat-car—so-called piggyback—equipment.

[20] See also Table 4.
[21] The writer's computation has been made from data supplied by Salomon Bros. & Hutzler.

*CHAPTER X*

# Conclusion

WHAT of the future? Are equipment trust certificates, conditional sale contracts, and lease plans likely to remain the principal vehicles of railroad equipment financing, or are some or all of these likely to disappear? What are the implications of the Symes proposal for a government agency to lease equipment to the railroads? Does the proposal signalize the breakdown or inadequacy of present methods and, if adopted, would it supersede those methods?

Equipment trust certificates appear to have lost none of their popularity with railroads or investors. In 1956 and again in 1957 such issues exceeded $330 million, which was more than in any previous year except in 1948 and 1949.[1] These two years were periods of extraordinarily heavy capital expenditures on equipment,[2] and as usual the railroads found equipment trust certificates the cheapest method of financing, despite rising interest rates;

[1] 1956–58 data supplied by Salomon Bros. & Hutzler; earlier years from U.S. Interstate Commerce Commission, *Statistics of Railways in the United States,* published annually.

[2] $824 million in 1956 and $1,017 million in 1957, according to *Trends in Railroad Operations* (Washington, D.C., Bureau of Railway Economics, Association of American Railroads, December, 1957), Table 18.

## Conclusion

in 1958, when equipment expenditures fell below $500 million, sale of equipment trust certificates still exceeded $158 million. The approximate interest cost on the financing averaged 3.88 percent in 1956 and 4.29 percent in 1957, as compared with 3.01 percent in 1955, 3.23 percent in 1953, and less than 3 percent in other years subsequent to 1957,[3] but 1957 was a period when the United States Treasury was borrowing at rates up to 4.17 percent,[4] and new public utility bonds of the highest standing were offered at rates up to 4.85 percent.[5] Interest costs dropped sharply with the easing of money rates at the end of the year; only one of fourteen issues between the middle of December, 1957, and the middle of February, 1958, involved an interest cost above 4 percent.[6] Any obstacle to continued use of equipment trust financing lies less in interest costs, which continue as low as can be expected in relation to other money rates, than in the burden of the 20 percent down payment, which may be a serious drain on limited cash resources.

The roads which can not or will not make the necessary down payment may turn to conditional sale contracts, or to leases.[7] The former can sometimes be negotiated with

[3] 1956–57 averages computed from data supplied by Salomon Bros. & Hutzler; earlier years from *Statistics of Railways*.

[4] On $1,750 million Treasury bills due April 15, 1958, offered August 14, 1957; note also offering the previous month of 4 percent one-year certificate of indebtedness due August 1, 1958, and of 4 percent four-year Treasury notes due August 1, 1961.

[5] E.g., $70 million Southern Bell Telephone 5 percent Debentures due 1986, rated Aaa, offered June 18, 1957, at 102.86 to yield 4.85 percent.

[6] Data from Salomon Bros. & Hutzler.

[7] See above, Chapters VII and VIII.

little or no down payment; the latter habitually involve none. From this circumstance and from their lack of negotiability, both generally command higher interest rates than do equipment trust certificates; whether this higher direct cost will be offset by earnings to be realized from the cash which would otherwise be needed as a down payment, or by tax advantages,[8] is a question to be carefully weighed by those charged with the financing. Indications are that conditional sale financing continued heavy in both 1956 and 1957, and that lease arrangements took on new importance.[9] Each of those methods of financing seems to meet a real need and to have a proper place in the financial picture, but there is no present evidence that either can be expected to crowd out the other or to supersede equipment trust certificates.

The criticism has been made that equipment financing has become excessively popular and that equipment obligations, representing more than a quarter of the outstanding funded debt of American railroads, cannot be in as strong a position as they were a generation ago, when they represented a much smaller fraction.[10] There is an element of truth in this, for if one takes the extreme case of the railroad which has no other debt, it is evident that, in the event of financial difficulty, any reduction of debt and charges can be effected only at the expense of the equipment creditors, whose safety therefore (if one assumes that earnings cannot be increased sufficiently to

[8] See above, Chapter III, closing paragraphs.
[9] See above, Chapter VIII.   [10] See above, Table 3.

## Conclusion

carry the debt) lies only in their ability to repossess the equipment and sell it elsewhere. However, both in this case and in the more common case where equipment debt represents but a fraction, large or small, of the total debt, we must expect any bankruptcy trustee to survey all outstanding contracts and agreements with a view to determining which of them can advantageously be rejected.[11] If a particular contract can be rejected advantageously, it will presumably be disowned whether or not the company has other equipment obligation outstanding; on the other hand, if the value and earning power of the equipment under the contract are such that the trustee cannot afford to let it go, he will presumably "adopt" that particular contract, whatever the other obligations. In other words, if and when we reach the point where the equipment creditor must look to his equipment rather than to the general credit of the road, the vital point is the strength of his particular issue rather than of the equipment debt in general. The investor must insure the strength of his investment by insistence on down payments, retirement schedules, and types of equipment which will maintain adequate protection for the debt.

The Symes proposal for a government agency to acquire equipment and lease it to the railroads [12] proceeds

[11] See above, Chapter IV.

[12] See above, Chapter VIII, closing pages. The proposal is developed at some length on pages 52–68 of an exhibit accompanying Mr. Symes's testimony before the Surface Transportation Subcommittee, Senate Committee on Interstate and Foreign Commerce, at Washington on January 13, 1958. Substantially the same material has been pre-

from the basic premise that, to modernize the freight car fleet and eliminate car shortages, the railroads in the aggregate should buy at least 100,000 freight cars annually for the next ten years—a figure which is about twice the average of the preceding five years, and which involves "in terms of 1957 dollars, and including costs for the additional motive power needed to move them . . . over a billion dollars a year." [13] Having thus established a need well above that of postwar years, he then argues that it cannot be financed as that need has been. He asserts that a market cannot be found for equipment obligations in the necessary amounts, that depreciation is inadequate because the cars being replaced cost less than one third as much as those now being purchased,[14] that substantially no surplus earnings are available,[15] that at current interest rates the cost of borrowing is prohibitive except for the strongest roads, and that reduced working capital [16] will no longer permit cash purchases or down payments on installment purchases.

The first of these arguments is not convincing. A market can be found for equipment obligations as readily as

---

sented to various groups on behalf of The Pennsylvania Railroad Company by Mr. P. D. Fox, Assistant Vice President—Finance, who has been kind enough to give me a copy of his presentation.

[13] Subsequently mentioned on page 58 of the Symes exhibit as "New equipment in the range of one billion to one and one-half billion dollars a year."

[14] Presumably amortization of defense projects (see above, p. 3) helped to fill this gap during part of the postwar period.

[15] Earnings for 1958 were the poorest since 1946.

[16] For Class 1 railroads in the aggregate, net working capital declined from $1,643 million at the end of 1945 to $537 million on September 30, 1957 (*Trends in Railroad Operations*, Table 3).

## Conclusion

for the obligations of a government agency whose only revenue is from the lease of equipment to railroads presumably of inferior credit.[17] Nor is the point relating to interest rates convincing. Interest rates were high in 1957, but by no means prohibitive, and can be expected to reflect, as in the early months of 1958, any decline in the general level of interest rates.

The other arguments appear to have more merit. The proposed agency might be an effective means of subsidizing those roads which cannot finance their equipment otherwise. If the agency is to supply *"all"* [18] railroads, Mr. Symes's confidence that it would cost the government nothing does not seem warranted. On the other hand, the leases would not be cheap financing; [19] as an unguaranteed obligation dependent on rather doubtful revenues, the borrowing would not command government rates, and there is no reason to suppose that agency funds would supersede other forms of equipment financing. So far as one can judge at this time, the proposal is merely one of several which, if enacted into law, might ease the dif-

---

[17] Symes, on page 54 of his exhibit, states specifically "TERMS ARE LESS ATTRACTIVE to a railroad, financially, than conventional methods . . . *where such types of financing are available,"* and on page 61:

*"The top third* of the industry (financially) would continue to use cash and conventional financing where available—and would lease very little equipment from the government agency.

*"The middle third* of the industry would use conventional financing for as much new equipment as they could afford and lease the rest through the agency.

*"The bottom third* would have to rely almost entirely on leasing through the agency. . . ."

[18] Symes, exhibit, p. 61.   [19] *Ibid.;* also p. 60.

ficulties and facilitate the financing of the railroads. It is by no means the most fundamental, or least controversial, of such proposals. It is not an indictment or abandonment of established financing methods, but simply a recognition that in certain cases, which seem more important to some of the eastern roads than to those in the the south and west, the established methods may need to be supplemented.

APPENDIX A

# Form of Trust Certificate

$1,000                                     No.

## THE ALABAMA GREAT SOUTHERN RAILROAD EQUIPMENT TRUST, SERIES K

Equipment Trust Certificate
Total Authorized Issue $2,400,000

THE FIRST NATIONAL BANK OF BIRMINGHAM, Trustee
Dividends at the Rate of $4\frac{3}{8}\%$ Per Annum Payable

June 15 and December 15

Principal hereof payable              , 19

THE FIRST NATIONAL BANK OF BIRMINGHAM, as Trustee under an Equipment Trust Agreement dated as of June 15, 1957, between THE FIRST NATIONAL BANK OF BIRMINGHAM, Trustee, and THE ALABAMA GREAT SOUTHERN RAILROAD COMPANY (hereinafter called the Company), hereby certifies that the bearer, or, if this Certificate is registered as to principal, the registered holder hereof, is entitled to an interest in the principal amount of $1,000 in THE ALABAMA GREAT SOUTHERN RAILROAD EQUIPMENT TRUST, SERIES K, payable on       , 19   , upon presentation and surrender of this Certificate to the undersigned at its principal office in the City of Birmingham, State of Alabama, or at the option of the Bearer or registered holder, as the case may be, at the agency of the undersigned in the Borough of Manhattan, City and State of New York, and to payment, until said last mentioned date, of dividends on said principal amount at the rate of $4\frac{3}{8}\%$ per annum from June 15, 1957, semi-annually on June 15 and December 15 in each year, according to the tenor of the dividend warrants hereto annexed, upon presentation and surrender of such warrants, as they severally mature, to the undersigned at its said office, with interest at 6% on any unpaid principal and on any unpaid dividends to the extent that it shall be legally enforceable, all in such coin or currency of the United States of America as at the time of payment shall be legal tender for the payment of public and private debts, but payable only out of rentals or other moneys received by the undersigned and applicable to such payment under the provisions of said Agreement.

This Certificate is one of an issue of Certificates each of the principal amount of $1,000, and having an aggregate principal amount not exceeding $2,400,000, all of which are substantially similar except as to serial number and date of maturity, all issued or to be issued under and subject to the terms of said Agreement, under which certain railroad equipment leased to the Company (or cash or direct obligations of the United States of America in lieu thereof, as provided in said Agreement) is held by the undersigned in trust for the benefit of the holders of the interests represented by said Certificates, to which Agreement (a copy of which is on file with the undersigned at its principal office in the City of Birmingham, State of Alabama) reference is made for a full statement of the rights and obligations of the Company, the duties and immunities of the undersigned and the rights of the holder hereof thereunder.

This Certificate may be registered as to principal at the said office of the undersigned in the City of Birmingham, State of Alabama, or, at the option of the bearer or registered holder, as the case may be, at the agency of the undersigned in the Borough of Manhattan, City and State of New York, in the name of the holder thereof, and such registration noted hereon by or on behalf of the undersigned. Thereafter title

## Appendix A

to the interest represented by this Certificate shall pass only by transfer registered at said office or agency unless and until a transfer to bearer shall have been similarly registered and noted hereon. Such registration shall apply only to the principal of this Certificate and not to the dividend warrants hereunto attached, which shall continue to be payable to bearer and transferable by delivery.

Every taker and holder of this Certificate and of the attached warrants, by accepting the same, agrees with the undersigned, with the Company and with every subsequent taker and holder hereof and thereof that this Certificate (unless registered in the name of the holder) and such warrants shall be transferable with the same effect as in the case of a negotiable instrument payable to bearer, by delivery by any person having possession of the same, however such possession may have been acquired; and the undersigned and the Company may treat the bearer of this Certificate, or the registered holder hereof if this certificate be registered in his name as above provided, and the bearer of any dividend warrant attached hereto whether or not this Certificate be so registered, as the absolute owner of this Certificate or of said warrants, as the case may be, for all purposes, and shall not be affected by any notice to the contrary.

In case of default in the performance or observance of any of the covenants of the Company in said Agreement contained, the principal amount represented by this Certificate may be declared due and payable, as provided in said Agreement.

Neither this Certificate nor the dividend warrants attached hereto shall be deemed in any wise a promise to pay of the undersigned.

IN WITNESS WHEREOF, THE FIRST NATIONAL BANK OF BIRMINGHAM, Trustee, has caused this Certificate to be signed by the facsimile signature of one of its Executive Vice Presidents and its corporate seal, in facsimile, to be hereunto affixed and to be attested by one of its Trust Officers, and has caused dividend warrants bearing the facsimile signature of its Cashier to be attached hereto, as of the 15th day of June, 1957.

THE FIRST NATIONAL BANK OF BIRMINGHAM,<br>Trustee,

By ......................................
Executive Vice President

L.S.
ATTEST:

..................................
Trust Officer

APPENDIX B

# Form of Dividend Warrant

$............  No. ............

Due to the bearer hereof on the fifteenth day of 19    , on surrender hereof at the principal office of the undersigned in the City of Birmingham, State of Alabama, or at the option of the bearer, at the agency of the undersigned in the Borough of Manhattan, City and State of New York, $       , being the semi-annual dividend then due on Certificate No.      of THE ALABAMA GREAT SOUTHERN RAILROAD EQUIPMENT TRUST, SERIES K, payable only out of rentals or other moneys received by the undersigned and applicable to such payment under the provisions of the Equipment Trust Agreement dated as of June 15, 1957, referred to in said Certificate and as therein provided.

THE FIRST NATIONAL BANK OF BIRMINGHAM,
Trustee,
By .....................................
Cashier

APPENDIX C

## *Form of Guaranty*

THE ALABAMA GREAT SOUTHERN RAILROAD COMPANY, for a valuable consideration, hereby unconditionally guarantees to the bearer or registered holder of the within Certificate, and to the bearer or bearers of the dividend warrants appertaining thereto, the prompt payment of the principal of said Certificate, and of the dividends thereon specified in the dividend warrants thereto attached, with interest at 6% on any unpaid principal and on any unpaid dividends to the extent that it shall be legally enforceable, in accordance with the terms of said Certificate and the Equipment Trust Agreement referred to therein.

      THE ALABAMA GREAT SOUTHERN
      RAILROAD COMPANY
      By ...................................
            Vice President

APPENDIX D

# *Form of Circular on Equipment Trust*

$1,335,000
CHICAGO AND NORTH WESTERN RAILWAY
COMPANY EQUIPMENT TRUST OF 1957

5½% EQUIPMENT TRUST CERTIFICATES
(Philadelphia Plan)

To be dated March 15, 1957

To mature annually $89,000 on each March 15, 1958 to 1972, inclusive

To be guaranteed unconditionally as to par value and dividends by endorsement by Chicago and North Western Railway Company

Par value and semi-annual dividends (March 15 and September 15) payable in Chicago, Illinois. Definitive Certificates in dividend form in the denomination of $1,000 registerable as to par value. Not redeemable prior to maturity.

Issuance and sale of these Certificates are subject to authorization by the Interstate Commerce Commission.

The Certificates are to be issued under an agreement dated March 15, 1957 which provides for the issuance of $1,335,000

*Appendix D*

par value of Certificates to be secured by the following standard-gauge railroad equipment to cost not less than $1,907,143:

12 1750 H.P. diesel electric road switching locomotives, General Motors model designation GP-9.

These locomotive units are being built in accordance with General Motors locomotive specifications for new model designation GP-9 diesel electric locomotives, except that certain reusable components of General Motors model designation F-3 units are being remanufactured to GP-9 specifications and incorporated into the new GP-9 carbodies. The current purchase price for such GP-9 locomotives, with certain remanufactured components, is approximately 90% of that of GP-9 locomotives which do not include remanufactured components. Each of the twelve GP-9 locomotives delivered under this Trust will be sold under General Motors' standard warranty for new equipment which guarantees any part or parts of all units of equipment to be free from defect in material and workmanship under normal use and service for one year after delivery, or for 100,000 miles of scheduled service, whichever occurs first. Simultaneously with this transaction, the Company is selling to General Motors for approximately $578,000 twelve General Motors model designation F-3 diesel electric locomotives acquired by Chicago and North Western in 1947, some of the components of which, when remanufactured, may be used in the locomotives to be delivered under this Trust.

The aggregate par value of these Certificates will not exceed 70% of the actual cost of the specifically described equipment and any substituted or additional equipment, other than passenger or work equipment, subjected to this Trust. Deposited cash shall, upon request of the Company and upon the terms stated in the Agreement, be invested in United States Government securities.

Title to the equipment is to be vested in the Trustee and

*Appendix D*

the equipment leased to the Chicago and North Western Railway Company at a rental sufficient to pay the par value of the Certificates and the dividend warrants as they mature and other charges.

## MATURITIES AND YIELDS

| 1958 .... 4.75% | 1960 .... 5.20% | 1962 .... 5.40% |
| 1959 .... 5.00 | 1961 .... 5.30 | 1963–72 . 5.50 |

HALSEY, STUART & CO. INC.

DICK & MERLE-SMITH      R. W. PRESSPRICH & CO.

FREEMAN & COMPANY    MCMASTER HUTCHINSON & CO.

These Certificates are offered for delivery when, as and if received by us. Certificates in temporary or definitive form will be delivered at the office of Halsey, Stuart & Co. Inc., 123 South La Salle Street, Chicago, Illinois.

The information contained herein has been carefully compiled from sources considered reliable, including a letter of the Company dated February 27, 1957, and, while not guaranteed as to completeness or accuracy, we believe it to be correct as of this date.

N.Y. 2/27/57

# Index

Adkins, Leonard D., 85n
Agency agreement, provisions of, 117-21
Air lines, equipment obligations of, protection for, 51
Alabama Great Southern Railroad, 96n; Series K, 90n
Alco Products, Inc., lease plan, 131-32; lease and agreement with Pennsylvania Railroad, and assignments to American Locomotive and Equipment Company (subsidiary) and to Guaranty Trust Company of New York as agent, 131n
Alton Railroad, 76
American Car and Foundry Company and Guaranty Trust Company of New York agreement and assignment (1954), 117n
American Loan & Trust Co., Kneeland v., 56n
American Locomotive and Equipment Company, 131n
American Locomotive Company, see Alco Products
Amortization of defense projects, 42n; defined, 3

Andrews, Fidelity & Deposit Co. of Md. v., 91n
Ann Arbor Railroad, 76; Series C, 90n
Assignment, see Conditional sale contract, assignment
Assignment of equipment to single representative of lenders, advantages of, 122-23
Association of American Railroads, 101
Association of Life Insurance Counsel, 49
Atchison, Topeka and Santa Fe Railroad, 71n
Atlanta, Birmingham and Atlantic Railway, 35n, 75
Atlantic Coast Line Railroad, 32; and The First National City Bank of New York agreement (1956), cited, 113; supplemental agreement (1956), 112n, 122n

Bailment, defined, 23n
Baltimore and Ohio Railroad, 37, 40, 71 and n, 76

Baltimore and Susquehanna Rail Road Company, 21
Bangor and Aroostook Railroad, 37, 76, 94n; agreement (1954), 112n, 122n
Bankers Trust Company, 37
Banking Act of 1935, cited, 143
Banking Law (New York), Section 235, quoted, 68
Bankruptcy Act, obstacles to enforcement of mortgage liens, 18n; Section 77, quoted, 28; Section 77(b), cited, 54; Section 77, subsection (j), amendment to, quoted and discussed, 50
Bankruptcy trustee, and equipment trust agreement, 56 58
Bessemer and Lake Erie Equipment Trust of 1940, 145
"Best Friend of Charleston, The," pioneer American locomotive, 21
Blair, Rollins and Company, 143n
Borrower, conveniences to, of conditional sale contracts, 29-30; of private placements, 142-44
Boston and Maine Railroad, 140-41
Buffalo and Susquehanna Railway, 72-73, 81
Builder, definition of, 105n
Burlington, see Chicago, Burlington and Quincy Railroad

Call price, see Call provisions
Call provisions, defined, 91; in equipment trust certificates, 91-93; in conditional sale contracts, 111-13

Canada, equipment obligations in, 14
Canadian National Railway, equipment obligations, 14
Canadian Pacific Railway, equipment obligations, 14
Capital expenditures on equipment, in 1921–55 (table), 4; in 1956–57, 150 and n; in 1958, 151; and equipment obligations sold, ratio between (table), 7
Central of Georgia Railway, 76
Central Railroad of New Jersey, 76
Central Vermont Railway, 71
Certificates, and notes, Interstate Commerce Commission authorization of, 58-60; outstanding, ratio to original cost of equipment (table), 98
Charleston and Western Carolina Railway, agreement (1949), 112n, 122n, 123n
Chattel mortgage, 28, 52
Chesapeake and Ohio Railway, 33n, 94, 140
Chicago and Alton Railroad, 76
Chicago and Eastern Illinois Railroad, 75, 76
Chicago and North Western Railway, 76; Equipment Trust Certificates, 99-100; qualification of rebuilt units as "new," 100-1; cost of issues sold during 1956, 140
Chicago, Burlington and Quincy Railroad, 62, 140
Chicago Great Western Railway, 76
Chicago, Indianapolis and Louisville Railway, 76, 102

# Index

Chicago, Milwaukee and St. Paul Railway, 71
Chicago, Milwaukee, St. Paul and Pacific Railroad, 79
Chicago, Peoria and St. Louis Railroad, 74
Chicago, Rock Island and Pacific Railway Company, 33n, 38, 71; experience of equipment creditors, 35n, 71, 79, 81; petition for reorganization, June 7, 1933, 48-51; *In re,* 49 and n; General Counsel, quoted, 49n; Continental Illinois National Bank and Trust Company v., 294 U.S. 648 (1935), 50 and n; 1957 series, 94n; Series P, 96n; Series Q, 96n
Cincinnati, New Orleans and Texas Pacific Railway, 96n; Series L, 90n
Circuit Court of Appeals, concerning appeal by bondholders *in re* New York, Ontario and Western Railroad, quoted, 54-55
Clark, Edward W., 23
Clayton Act, Section 10, cited, 58
Colpitts, W. W., 38
Competitive bidding, preferred and eventually required by Interstate Commerce Commission, 60-62, 135; procedure, 135-36
Concessions, defined, 138
Conditional Sale Agreement by and between Pullman-Standard Car Manufacturing Company and The Kansas City Southern Railway Company (1956), quoted, 107

Conditional sale contracts, 29-35, 104-23; increasing importance, 29, reasons for, 29-30; versus equipment trust agreements, 62; freedom from Interstate Commerce Commission jurisdiction, 62-64; Interstate Commerce Commission recommendations for legislation conferring jurisdiction, 64-65; Public Service Commission of New York asserts jurisdiction, 65-66; compared with equipment trust agreements, 104-5; analysis of, 105-23; assignment, provisions of, 115-17; advantages of, 151-52
Conditional sale plan, 25-26
Continental Illinois National Bank and Trust Company v. Chicago, Rock Island and Pacific Railway, 294 U.S. 648 (1935), 50 and n
County Transportation, 66 and n
Coverdale and Colpitts, 38
Cravath, Swaine & Moore, 85n
Credit, borrower's, as factor in marketing of equipment obligations, 139-42

Davis Polk Wardwell Sunderland & Kiendl, 85n; letter to Department of Banking, State of New York, quoted, 101
Debt, total railroad, compared with equipment obligations outstanding, 8-11
Default, defined, 114; cases reviewed, 69-81

Delaware and Hudson Railroad, 66
Delaware, Lackawanna and Western Railroad, opposition to Symes proposal, 134
Denver and Rio Grande Railroad, default on equipment obligations, 1885, 17$n$; reorganization, 69-70, 81
Denver and Rio Grande Western Railroad, 71, 76, 140
Depreciation, defined, 3; accelerated, 42$n$
Detroit Southern Railroad, 72
Detroit, Toledo and Ironton Railway, 72, 81
Dewing, Arthur Stone, *A Study of Corporation Securities,* cited, 28, 77; quoted, 19, 27, 69, 71, 72-73, 73-74
Dick & Merle-Smith, 100$n$
Diesel-electric power, substituted for steam, 9
Director General of Railroads, annual report, 1922, quoted, 34; annual report, 1924, cited, 34; annual report, 1932, quoted, 34
Dividend warrant, form of, 161
Down payments and maturity schedules, 93-95, 96-98, 121-22, and 122$n$
Duncan, Kenneth, *Equipment Obligations,* cited, 8, 26, 27, 35, 38, 72, 73, 74, 75, 85$n$; quoted, 44-45, 46

Eastman, Joseph Bartlett, quoted, 60
Electro-motive Division, General Motors Corporation, 98$n$, 99

Equipment, capital expenditures on, in 1921-1955 (table), 4; in 1956-1957, 150 and $n$; in 1958, 151; reservation of title to, by lease or conditional sale, 18-20; Canadian provision for lien on, before delivery, 28; conversion of, 98-99; definition of, 1, 86-87; rebuilding of, 98-99
Equipment bonds, weakness of, 27-29
Equipment creditor, right of repossession fortified by statute, 50-51; confirmed by court, 54-56
Equipment expenditures, size of, 2-14
Equipment financing, growth of, 1-14; distinctive, reasons for, 15-20; average rate on less than on other debt financing, 18$n$, interest cost of, 140-41, 150-51, 154-55; first distinctive use of, 21; history of, 21-43; criticisms of, 152-53
Equipment obligations, defined, 2; of United States railways, 1921-1955 (table), 4, (table), 6; sold, and capital expenditures on equipment, ratio between, 6 (table), 7; outstanding, compared with total railroad debt, 8-9, (table), 10-11; U.S. government experience with, 32-35; U.S. government sale of, 32-35; legal status of, 44-68; relatively riskless investments, 69-82; probability of punctual payment, 82; marketing of, 135-49, borrower's credit as factor in, 139-42, na-

# Index

ture of equipment as factor in, 149; pricing of, 136-41; private placement of, 142-44; secondary markets for, 146-49; secondary to government obligations, 147

Equipment purchases, special corporations for financing, 35-36

Equipment trust agreements, 83-103; and bankruptcy trustee, 56-58; executed in new form in 1957, 90n; status under Negotiable Instrument Law, 91

Equipment trust certificates, issued against equipment built from reworked parts but qualified as "new," 99-101; issued against equipment which does not qualify as "new," 102-3; market for, chiefly among institutional investors, 142; private placement of, 142-44; continued popularity of, 150-51; form of, 157-60

Equipment trust circular, form of, 163-65

Equipment Trusts of January 15, 1920 (to United States Railroad Administration), 25-26, 91; issue, 31-32; government experience with resale, collection, 32-34; factors in resale, 34-35; investor experience, 35

Equipment unit, fair value, definition of, 87

Equitable Life Assurance Society, lease plan, 9-12, 19-20, 124-27

Erie Railroad, 71n, 76

Federal Emergency Administration of Public Works, 103

Fidelity & Deposit Co. of Md. v. Andrews, 91n

First lien on rolling stock, advantages of, 17-20

First mortgage, inability of typical railroad to use as security for equipment purchases, 15-16

First mortgage bonds, factors affecting value of, 16

First National Bank of Dallas, 143

First National City Bank of New York, The, and Atlantic Coast Line agreement (1956), cited, 113

FitzGibbon, Thomas O'G., 85n; quoted, 86n

Florida East Coast Railway, 18n, 79-80, 81, 82

Freeman, Lewis D., et al., United States of America, Plaintiff vs., 80n

Freight cars, probable expenditures for, 9; limited advantages in ownership of, 39-40; suggestions for special financing arrangements for, 39-40

Fruit Growers Express Company, 14n

Funded debt and equipment obligations outstanding, compared (table), 10-11

General American Transportation Corporation, 14n

General Motors Corporation, 98-99, 98n, 101; urges replacement rather than overhauling

General Motors Corp. (*Cont.*) of older units, 9, 98-99; warranty, quoted, 100; and Southern Pacific Company agreement (1956), 113n; lease plan, 131-32
Gerstenberg, Charles W., *Materials of Corporation Finance*, cited, 85n
Gibb, George S., cited, 21-22
Gibbons, Charles, 23
Government Equipment Trusts of January 15, 1920, *see* Equipment Trusts of January 15, 1920
Gross capital expenditures of United States railways, 1921–1955 (table), 4; compared with certain sources of funds (table), 6
Guaranty, form of, 162
Guaranty Trust Company of New York, 31, 35, 37, 131n; and American Car and Foundry Company agreement and assignment (1954), 117n
Gulf, Mobile and Ohio Railroad, Series H, 90n; 1952 series, 95n

Halsey, Stuart & Co., 100, 136, 143n
Hanover Bank, The, 53
Hoboken R. Co., Smith v., decision cited, 54; Circuit Court of Appeals opinion on, 54-55
Holder of equipment obligations, protection of, 17-20

Ideal Laundry, *In re*, 51n
Illinois Central Railroad, 102-3
Illinois Terminal Railroad, 94n
Income tax rates, influence on leasing plans, 41-42
Indianapolis, B. & W. Ry., Turner v., 56n
Insurance Law (New York), Section 81(4)b, quoted, 68
Interest cost of equipment financing, 18n, 140-41, 150-51, 154-55
Interest curve, 145-46; defined, 145
International Great Northern Railroad, 76
Interstate Commerce Act, Section 20(a), 7-8, quoted, 58-59; Section 20b, quoted, 51; Section 20c, quoted, 46-47; advantages of 20c discussed, 47-48
Interstate Commerce Commission, 36, 37, 58, 92, 94, 135, 144; given jurisdiction over issue of carrier securities, 7-8; authorization of notes and certificates, 58-60; preference and eventual requirement for competitive bidding on equipment trust certificates, 60-62; recommendations for legislation conferring jurisdiction over conditional sale contracts and leases, 64-65; 66th Annual Report (1952), quoted, 64-65; 70th Annual Report (1956), quoted, 65
Investors, experience with purchase of government-sold obligations, 35; interest in punctuality as well as eventual safety of payment, 81-82, 141-42; institutional, as buyers for equipment trust certificates,

# Index

142; necessity for insistence on adequate protection, 153

Kansas City Southern Railway and The New York Trust Company, agreement (1956), 118n, 122n
Kenan, New York Trust Co. v., 56n
Kidder, Peabody and Company, 143n
Kneeland v. American Loan & Trust Co., 56n
Kuhn, Loeb and Company, 32

Lake's Laundry, Inc., *In re,* 50n
Lane v. Macon & A. Ry., 56n
Lease plan, Equitable Life Assurance Society, brief outline, 9-12; sum financed, 12; provisions of, 124-27
Lease plan, National Equipment Leasing Corporation, provisions of, 127-31
Leases, bona fide, advantages of, 40-42, 128, 151-52; influence of income tax rates on, 41-42; Interstate Commerce Commission recommendations for legislation conferring jurisdiction over, 64-65; defined and distinguished from leases in Philadelphia Plan, 124; outlined, 124-34
Leases, under Philadelphia Plan, origin and use of, 23-25; provisions of, 83-84; combination into trust agreement, 86-91
Lehigh Coal and Navigation Company, 23

Lehigh Valley Railroad, 63, 76
Lenders, able and willing to dispense with negotiability, emergence of, 30
Locks and Canals Company, Lowell, Mass., 21
Locomotives, advantages in ownership of, 39
Long Island Rail Road, 76
Louisville and Nashville Railroad, 32; agreement (1952), cited, 108; 112 and n, 122n; letter to Guaranty Trust Company of New York, cited, 114 and n

Macon & A. Ry., Lane v., 56n
Mahaffie Act, *see* Interstate Commerce Act, Section 20b
Marketability, 146-49
Masson, Robert L., and Samuel S. Stratton, *Financial Instruments and Institutions: A Case Book,* cited, 85n
Maturity schedules, 95-99, 121-22; and down payment, effect of variations, 96-98; shortening of, in consequence of rebuilding equipment, 98-101
Mercantile Trust Company and Lenders named [in connection with St. Louis-San Francisco Railway Company] agreement (1957), 118n, quoted, 120
Merchants Despatch, 14n
Missouri, Kansas and Texas Railway, 71
Missouri Pacific Railroad, 71, 78
Minneapolis and St. Louis Railway Company, 34, 35, 38, 76
Mobile and Ohio Railroad, 78-79

Monon, *see* Chicago, Indianapolis and Louisville Railway
Mortgage, *see* Chattel mortgage; Equipment bonds; First lien on rolling stock; First mortgage; Purchase money mortgage
Moynahan, John J., quoted, 101

Narrow gauge equipment, disadvantages of, 17*n*, 70
National Association of Owners of Railroad Securities, 36
National Equipment Leasing Corporation, 149; lease plan, 127-31; —, *When Does It Pay to LEASE Equipment?*, quoted, 128
National Railway Service Corporation, 36-40
Negotiable Instrument Law, status of equipment trust certificates under, 91
New Haven, *see* New York, New Haven and Hartford Railroad
New Orleans, Texas and Mexico Railway, 37, 76
New York Banking Law, Section 235, quoted, 68; subdivision 7(c), cited, 95*n*, 100
New York Central Lines Equipment Trust of 1925, 60 and *n*
New York Central Railroad, 32, 60, 67, 135*n*; mortgages, 15; protests against Public Service Commission of New York jurisdiction, quoted, 66; protests overruled, 66
New York, Chicago and St. Louis Second Equipment Trust of 1956, 139

New York Insurance Law, Section 81(4)b, quoted, 68
New York, New Haven and Hartford Railroad, 76, 95, 140; Equipment Trust of 1956 #2, 139
New York, Ontario and Western Railroad, 18*n*, 80, 81, and Reconstruction Finance Corporation, 52-56; 1945 trust, 82
New York Personal Property Law, Sections 260-262, cited, 91*n*
New York Plan, 25-27
New York State, Banking Department, statement on "remanufactured" equipment, quoted, 101
New York Trust Co. v. Kenan, 56*n*; and corporation and trusts named in Schedule A [in connection with Kansas City Southern Railway], agreement (1956), 118*n*; and twelve other lenders, and Southern Pacific Railroad, agreement (1956), 120*n*
Norfolk and Western Railroad, 32, 81; reorganization of, 70-71; 1957 series, 94*n*
Norfolk Southern Railroad, 35*n*, 77-78; Equipment Trust of 1925, 60 and *n*
Northern Pacific Railroad, 32, 71*n*; North Western, *see* Chicago and North Western Railway
Notes, and certificates, Interstate Commerce Commission authorization of, 58-60

# Index

Ontario, see New York, Ontario and Western Railroad

Pacific Fruit Express Company, 14n

Pennsylvania, early decisions in, necessitating the Philadelphia Plan, 23-24

Pennsylvania Railroad, 31-32, 132; agreement (January 15, 1920), cited, 33; General Equipment Trust, Series D, 60 and n; 1955-1956 series, 94n; Conditional Sale Agreements, agreement (1952) of Philadelphia National Bank and other banks, insurance companies, and other lenders, relating to, quoted, 121; agreements and assignments to the Philadelphia National Bank (1952), 122n; and Alco Products Inc., lease and agreement, assignment to American Locomotive and Equipment Company (1957), 131n; and Alco Products Inc., lease and agreement, assignment to Guaranty Trust Company of New York (1957), 131n

Pere Marquette Railroad, 74

Philadelphia National Bank and other banks, insurance companies, and other lenders, agreement (1952), relating to Conditional Sale Agreements of The Pennsylvania Railroad Company, quoted, 121

Philadelphia Plan, 20 and n, 24-27, 31-32, 86n, 135; agreements under, 83-103

Philadelphia and Reading Railroad Company, 21; Platt v., 56n

Platt v. Philadelphia & R.R.R., 56n

Pointer Brewing Co., In re, 50n

Prepayment clauses, see Call provisions

Prepayment provisions, see Call provisions

Pressprich and Company, 143n

Pricing of equipment obligations, 136-46

Private car lines, ownership of rolling stock, 12-14

Private placement of equipment obligations, 29-30, 36, 138n, 142-44; exemption under Section 77 d(1) of Securities Act, 67; clause in agreements, 120-21

Prudential Insurance Company, 32

Public Law 85-295, quoted, 51n

Public Service Commission of New York, assumes jurisdiction over issuance of conditional sale contracts, 65-66; jurisdiction protested by New York Central Railroad, 66

Purchase money mortgage, 28

Railroad Car Trust of Philadelphia, 23

Railroad Motive Power and Equipment Act, 1919, 31

Railway Equipment Agency, federal, proposed by James M. Symes, 132-34, 153-56

Rawle, Francis, "Car Trust Se-

Rawle, Francis (*Continued*)
curities," cited, 8; quoted, 22-23, 23-24, 25, 27
Reading Series V, 94n
Receivership, and reorganization, 69-82; cases without default on equipment obligations, 71, 76
Reconstruction Finance Corporation, 103; and New York, Ontario and Western Railroad reorganization, 52-56
Reorganization, and receivership, 69-82; without default, 71, 76
Refrigerator cars, private ownership of, 12-13
Retirement, defined, 3
Revenue act, amended 1941 (Section 124), 3
Rock Island, *see* Chicago, Rock Island and Pacific Railway Company
Rolling stock, private ownership of, 12-14; first lien on, advantages of, 17-20; standard, defined, 17n

St. Louis, Brownsville and Mexico Railroad, 95
St. Louis-San Francisco Railway, 35n, 71, 78; agreements (1957), 113n; Lenders, and Mercantile Trust Company, agreement (1957), 113n, 118n, quoted, 120
Salomon Bros. & Hutzler, 136, 143n
Sargent, James C., cited, 92 and n
Sale contract (conditional), provisions of, 105-13
Schuykill Navigation Company, 22

Seaboard Air Line Railway, 35n, 36, 76-77, 81, 92; Series Q, 94n
Secondary markets, 146-49; for issues first privately placed, 147-49
Securities Act of 1933, 144; quoted, 67; limited application of registration provisions, 67, 147 and n
Securities and Exchange Commission, 36, 144
Shanks, Carroll, quoted, 49-50
Smith, Paul, Jr., The Development of the Legal Status of American Railroad Equipment Securities, cited, 8, 21, 25, 35, 36, 50, 56n, 59n, 68, 75, 91n, 94; quoted, 27, 28, 45
Smith v. Hoboken R. Co., decision cited, 54; Circuit Court of Appeals opinion on, 54-55
Southern Pacific Company, 95; Series JJ, through VV, 94; Series HH, 95n; Series II, 95n; and General Motors Corporation agreement (1956), 113n; and The New York Trust Company and twelve other lenders, agreement (1956), 120n; agreements (1956), 122n; Equipment Trust (1955), 145
Southern Railway, 96n; mortgage, 15-16; Series UU, 90n
Spread, gross, in cost of equipment obligations, 138-41
Stevenson, John, "Railroad Equipment Financing," cited, 77; quoted, 31, 123
Stratton, Samuel S., *see* Masson, Robert L.

# Index

Subsidiary corporations, ownership of rolling stock, 12-14
Symes, James M., proposal for a federal Railway Equipment Agency, 42-43, 132-34, 153-56; testimony before Surface Transportation Subcommittee, Senate Committee on Interstate and Foreign Commerce, exhibit, cited, 153, 154; quoted, 155*n*
Syndicates, purchase of equipment obligations by, 136-38

Tank cars, private ownership of, 12-13
Texas and Pacific Railway, 143
Texas-New Mexico Railway, 143
Thomas v. Western Car Co., 56*n*
Transportation Act of 1920, 58; Section 210, establishment of revolving fund, 37
Trust agreement, provisions of, 84-85; and lease, combination of, 86-91
Trust certificate, form of, 157-60
Turner v. Indianapolis, B. & W. Ry., 56*n*

Union Pacific Railroad, 60, 71*n*; Equipment Trust, Series D, 60 and *n*
U.S.C., 49, Section 1(18), 55; quoted, 55*n*

United States government, control and operation of railroads during First World War, 31-32; experience with equipment obligations, 32-35
United States of America, Plaintiff, vs. Lewis D. Freeman, Trustee *et al.*, 80*n*
United States Railroad Administration, 26
United States Supreme Court, 50
United States Treasury, bills, 145; certificates, 145; notes, 145

Virginian Railroad, 92

Wabash Railroad, 35*n*, 73, 77, 92; Series I, 90*n*
Warfield, S. Davies, 36
War Finance Corporation, 33
Western Car Co., Thomas v., 56*n*
Western Fruit Express, 14*n*
Western Pacific Railroad, 76
Wheeling and Lake Erie Railroad, 38, 73-74, 95
White Plains Ice Service, Inc., *In re,* 51*n*
Wilson & Co., Inc., agreement (1956), 112*n*, 122*n*
Wisconsin Central Railroad, 76
Woodlock, Thomas Francis, quoted, 60-61